Institutional Racism in America

EDITED BY

Louis L. Knowles

and

Kenneth Prewitt

CONTRIBUTORS:

Owen Blank
Jim Davis
Jacquelyn G. Drews
Paul Drews
Sue Haley
Andrew Horowitz
Louis L. Knowles
Sue Mithune
Kenneth Prewitt
Peter Ware

WITH AN APPENDIX BY

Harold Baron

Prentice-Hall, Inc. A SPECTRUM BOOK   *Englewood Cliffs, N. J.*

Current printing (last number):
10 9 8 7 6 5 4 3 2 1

PRENTICE-HALL INTERNATIONAL, INC. (*London*)
PRENTICE-HALL OF AUSTRALIA, PTY. LTD. (*Sydney*)
PRENTICE-HALL OF CANADA, LTD. (*Toronto*)
PRENTICE-HALL OF INDIA PRIVATE LIMITED (*New Delhi*)
PRENTICE-HALL OF JAPAN, INC. (*Tokyo*)

*Dedicated to the belief
that institutions are made by men
and can be changed by men.
—Let us be about the task.*

Preface

The description and analysis of institutional racism, which occupies the greater part of this book, is the product of a set of unusual educational circumstances. The Stanford chapter of the University Christian Movement, represented by Stuart McLean, in cooperation with the Mid-Peninsula Christian Ministry of East Palo Alto, California, under the leadership of the Reverend Carl Smith, designed a joint program that subsequently was dubbed a "work-study" seminar. A group of white Stanford students worked full-time for the Ministry in the summer of 1967. On a part-time basis, the group continued to assist the Ministry in its program and involvement in community issues throughout the academic year. In addition, during the academic year 1967–68, the students met weekly in a credit seminar with Peter Ware of the Ministry Staff and Professor Kenneth Prewitt, a political scientist visiting Stanford from the University of Chicago.

The Mid-Peninsula Christian Ministry is a white, church-funded, urban-oriented organization that took seriously the problem of white racism even before the Kerner Report popularized that term. The Ministry had already begun to move the center of its program to the white community when the student team arrived on the scene. In addition to traditional community services such as day camps for black children and assistance to those seeking employment, the Ministry for some time had sought to organize a white constituency with some political understanding of black power and white institutions. The student team assisted in speaking engagements and educational demonstrations, and attended countless community meetings in both black and white areas. During the year, most of us became personally involved with unresponsive school boards, housing commissions, and police agencies.

Simultaneously with our community work, we were engaged in a course of study. However, unlike many university programs that investigate social conflict at close range, the work-study team never had any pretensions to neutrality. Our work with the Ministry and our study in the seminar were based on the premise that black liberation overshadowed all other domestic issues and priorities. Indeed, we merged the "work" and the "study" as closely together as possible. Having assumed a basic political stance on the question of race, the team determined to evolve a strategy and set of tactics for social change in the white community. Although most of us lived in the black community of East Palo Alto, our attention was directed to the white communities across the Bayshore Freeway. Our daily contact with the movement for self-determination within the black community constantly renewed in us a sense of the urgent need for change in the white community. Living in the black community helped us see just how white institutions played games with black self-determination. At the same time we came increasingly to see how shallow and futile most white responses had been. We became convinced that effective white action could only come from intelligent and careful analysis of racism and its effect on both black and white people.

The main written products of the work-study team, found in the following pages, are a systematization and generalization of what we learned through study of institutional racism and through involvement in the struggle against the present white controlled institutional arrangements in American society. The book is not simply a dispassionate description of institutional racism, though we believe our account is an accurate one. We hope that it will persuade people that the critical struggle in America is the one directed against white racism and will provide people who have already engaged in that struggle, or are willing to do so, with some analytic tools to aid their progress.

It was probably the tension between a desire for action and change, on the one hand, and the difficulty of knowing *what* to do, on the other, that sparked whatever creativity the group possessed. Our participation in local conflicts kept these pressures alive in our minds at all times. The seminar meeting became the point at which a process of synthesis went on as we discussed the events of the preceding week and the many new books and articles on black power and racism which appeared during the year. We prepared working papers on issues related to institutional racism, papers which were designed to provide us with greater insight and to increase our political effectiveness. These papers became the basis for this book.*

The combination of living in the black community, being politically involved in the white community, and reading and writing about racism provided us with some insight into what it means to be poor, black, and without resources except your anger and that of your brother to throw against the commissioners, the supervisors, the chiefs, the rulers, all of whom have batteries of experts and reports to prove that your grievances are not real. At the same time, we became painfully aware that as white university students we were members of a privileged group with major resources at our disposal that were being used primarily *against* the black struggle for self-determination. The undergraduate student customarily fits into a prescribed program that supplies him with a well-defined and academically acceptable "body of knowledge." His education prepares him for a "career" and educational authorities "certify" that he is ready for the next step after four years of absorbing the cumulated, and conventional, wisdom. As students at a prestigious, private, and white university, we feared that the conventional wisdom we were acquiring, the certification process through which we were moving, and the careers for which we should have been preparing would only further strengthen the institutional arrangements in American society which penalized black people.

We wanted to utilize the resources of the university toward a different goal. We permitted the nature of the current community issues to determine the knowledge we felt we needed. For instance, inadequate educational programs were a constant source of irritation in the black community. Control of the schools was a hot political issue in both the white and the black communities. University faculty and the university library proved to be helpful as we sought a broader perspective on questions of busing, integrated classrooms, and related concerns. This broader perspective became a useful tool as we worked to organize and inform a white support block for black demands for better schooling. It is significant that this flow of in-

* Working papers prepared by students other than those involved in the work-study team, or by members who were not directly involved in preparing this manuscript, were of great help to us. Some of these papers came from seminars which were organized and sometimes taught by team members. We particularly want to acknowledge contributions by Kurt Schnepple, a member of the work-study team who left Stanford prior to the actual work on this book, Tory Mudd, Tina Press, Bob Cochrane, Barbara Ehrlich, Steve Cummings, and Carl Malgram.

formation occurred almost entirely *outside* the curricular framework
of the university. We refused to be programmed by the university;
rather we used it as a giant consulting firm for our group goals. This
arrangement led to a sense of self-direction and purpose in our education that surpassed anything we had known within the university
environment. This sense of self-direction in turn has helped us to
think more clearly about the careers in white institutions for which
a Stanford degree was presumably preparing us. We have rejected
these career lines and, both individually and collectively, are search-
ing for ways to make our education work against, rather than for,
racist institutions.

Our team members feel that we were successful in breaking
through some of the old barriers and creating some new educational
forms; but we also know that no black or poor groups are able to
use the university as we did. Such groups are denied access by most
present admission policies and by the alliance of university brain-
power with community elites. The intellectual and technological
powers of the university most often appear in community conflicts
as allies of the governing boards and large corporations. In fact, the
major universities have spawned a set of special firms such as the
Stanford Research Institute, the University of Chicago Center for
Urban Studies, and others that, as a major part of their work, study
social problems and seek solutions amenable to the preservation of
governing elites. Our experimental program was a step toward util-
ization of intellectual resources *against* the present constellations of
power.

From the exclusion by the university of minority racial and poverty groups have come the demands for unlimited black and Puerto
Rican admission and for departments of Third World and working-
class studies. As strange as these ideas sound to the ears of middle-
and upper-class whites, there is convincing evidence that higher
education must drastically alter its relationship to the poor and
lower-class communities. It is not enough to accept only the exceptional black student who has assimilated white norms, and then to
place him in a curriculum that has little or nothing to do with the
struggle for freedom in the black community. Higher education, if
it intends to remain a central force in our society, must provide resources in large quantities directly to the people and their community organizations, rather than skimming off the best minds for
private cultivation.

For those who are now within the academic community, the

work-study team members highly recommend experiments in the use of academic credit for work-study programs. As an alternative to dropping-out of higher education, students who see our social institutions as hypocritical should seek to re-order these institutions —in particular, the manner in which the university relates to society. Dramatic protest is one side of this movement toward new educational structures; the other side is the construction of new university-community ties through programs such as the work-study team. And we have found that an organizational revolt alone is insufficient: it is also necessary to re-think our understanding of American society. In this book we present the fruits of our "intellectual revolt," our struggle to define racism not as Negro Pathology, but as White and Institutional and all too American.

OWEN BLANK
JIM DAVIS
JACQUELYN G. DREWS
PAUL DREWS
SUE HALEY
ANDREW HOROWITZ
LOUIS L. KNOWLES
SUE MITHUNE
KENNETH PREWITT
PETER WARE

Contents

Chapter 1

Institutional and Ideological Roots of Racism

Racism is both overt and covert. It takes two, closely related forms: individual whites acting against individual blacks, and acts by the total white community against the black community. We call these individual racism and institutional racism. The first consists of overt acts by individuals, which cause death, injury or the violent destruction of property. This type can be reached by television cameras; it can frequently be observed in the process of commission. The second type is less overt, far more subtle, less identifiable in terms of specific individuals committing the acts. But it is no less destructive of human life. The second type originates in the operation of established and respected forces in the society, and thus receives far less public condemnation than the first type.

STOKELY CARMICHAEL AND CHARLES V. HAMILTON

Negroes in America have been subject to "victimization" in the sense that a system of social relations operates in such a way as to deprive them of a chance to share in the more desirable material and nonmaterial products of a society which is dependent, in part, upon their labor and loyalty. They are "victimized," also, because they do not have the same degree of access which others have to the attributes needed for rising in the general class system—money, education, "contacts," and "know-how."

ST. CLAIR DRAKE

What white Americans have never fully understood—but what the Negro can never forget—is that white society is deeply impli-

1

*cated in the ghetto. White institutions created it, white institutions
maintain it, and white society condones it.*

Report of the National Advisory
Commission on Civil Disorders

THE REPORT OF THE NATIONAL ADVISORY
COMMISSION ON CIVIL DISORDERS: A COMMENT

The contemporary document perhaps most indicative of the
ideology of official America is the influential "Kerner Commission
Report." This is an important work. It is being widely read, and we
cite from it frequently in the pages to follow. However, since our
analysis operates from a premise fundamentally different from the
Report, a few comments at this point will help introduce the substantive chapters to follow.

The Report asks: "Why Did It Happen?" A painful truth is then
recorded: "White racism is essentially responsible for the explosive
mixture which has been accumulating in our cities since the end of
World War II." Unfortunately, the Report too quickly leaves this
truth and emphasizes the familiar list of "conditions" of "Negro
unrest." Paraded before the reader are observations about the frustrated hopes of Negroes, the "belief" among Negroes that there is
police brutality, the high unemployment in the ghetto, the weak
family structure and social disorganization in the Negro community,
and so on.

It is the immediate conditions giving rise to civil disorders which
the Report stresses, not the *causes behind the conditions.* Perhaps
what is needed is a National Advisory Commission on White Racism. If a group of men sets out to investigate "civil disorders," their
categories of analysis are fixed and, from our perspective, parochial.
In spite of their admission that "white institutions created [the
ghetto], white institutions maintain it, and white society condones
it," the categories with which the commission operated screened out
the responsibility of white institutions and pushed the commission
back to the familiar account of "black pathology."

In the important section "What Can Be Done," this fault is even more clearly seen. Certainly it is true that much accumulated frustration would be relieved if the sweeping recommendations concerning administration of justice, police and community relations, housing, unemployment and underemployment, welfare thinking, and so forth were implemented. The Report merits the closest attention for its statement that issues of race and poverty must receive the highest national priority, and for its further argument that what is needed is a massive commitment by all segments of society. What disappoints the reader is that the section "What Can Be Done" only accentuates the shortsightedness of the section "Why Did It Happen." The recommendations are directed at ghetto conditions and *not* at the white structures and practices which are responsible for those conditions. Thus, while it is true that improved communication between the ghetto and city hall might defuse the pressures building up in the black community, the issue is not "better communication" but "full representation." Black people should not have to communicate with city hall; they should be represented at city hall.

The shallowness of the Report as social analysis is again reflected in its discussion of black protest movements. The Report does not uncover a critical social dynamic: militancy is first of all a response to white resistance and control, not its cause. The naiveté of the Report, and its ultimate paternalism, is nowhere better shown than in its attempt to draw parallels between the black power movement and the philosophy of Booker T. Washington. Accommodation stood at the center of Washington's thought; accommodation is explicitly and forcefully rejected by the ideology symbolized in the "black power" slogan. As Carmichael and Hamilton wrote, "Black people in the United States must raise hard questions which challenge the very nature of the society itself: its long-standing values, beliefs, and institutions."

What we miss in the Kerner Commission Report is the capacity to ask "hard questions." The Commission members are to be saluted for their instinct that "white racism" is the culprit. They are to be faulted for their inability or unwillingness to pursue this theme. We do not have access to the professional resources available to the Kerner Commission, and therefore our study lacks the statistical detail of the national report. But we have tried to push the analysis of the race question into areas where the Report dared not tread: into the heart of institutional, which is to say white, America.

A new realization is dawning in white America. Under the insistent prodding of articulate blacks plus a few unusual whites, the so-called "Negro Problem" is being redefined. Just possibly the racial sickness in our society is not, as we have so long assumed, rooted in the black and presumably "pathological" subculture but in the white and presumably "healthy" dominant culture. If indeed it turns out that "*the* problem" is finally and deeply a white problem, the solution will have to be found in a restructured white society.

Institutional racism is a term which describes practices in the United States nearly as old as the nation itself. The term, however, appears to be of recent coinage, possibly first used by Stokely Carmichael and Charles V. Hamilton in their widely read book, *Black Power*.[1] It is our goal to work with this term until we feel we have come to some full understanding of it, and to present an analysis of specific practices appropriately defined as "institutionally racist." Our strategy is to be self-consciously pragmatic. That is, we ask not what the motive of the individuals might be; rather we look at the consequences of the institutions they have created.

TOWARD A DEFINITION

The murder by KKK members and law enforcement officials of three civil rights workers in Mississippi was an act of individual racism. That the sovereign state of Mississippi refused to indict the killers was institutional racism. The individual act by racist bigots went unpunished in Mississippi because of policies, precedents, and practices that are an integral part of that state's legal institutions. A store clerk who suspects that black children in his store are there to steal candy but white children are there to purchase candy, and who treats the children differently, the blacks as probable delinquents and the whites as probable customers, also illustrates indi-

---

[1] Stokely Carmichael and Charles Hamilton, *Black Power: The Politics of Liberation in America* (New York: Vintage Books, 1967).

vidual racism. Unlike the Mississippi murderers, the store clerk is not a bigot and may not even consider himself prejudiced, but his behavior is shaped by racial stereotypes which have been part of his unconscious since childhood. A university admissions policy which provides for entrance only to students who score high on tests designed primarily for white suburban high schools necessarily excludes black ghetto-educated students. Unlike the legal policies of Mississippi, the university admission criteria are not intended to be racist, but the university is pursuing a course which perpetuates institutional racism. The difference, then, between individual and institutional racism is not a difference in intent or of visibility. Both the individual act of racism and the racist institutional policy may occur without the presence of conscious bigotry, and both may be masked intentionally or innocently.

In an attempt to understand "institutional racism" it is best to consider first what institutions are and what they do in a society. Institutions are fairly stable social arrangements and practices through which collective actions are taken. Medical institutions, for instance, marshal talents and resources of society so that health care can be provided. Medical institutions include hospitals, research labs, and clinics, as well as organizations of medical people such as doctors and nurses. The health of all of us is affected by general medical policies and by established practices and ethics. Business and labor, for example, determine what is to be produced, how it is to be produced, and by whom and on whose behalf products will be created. Public and private schools determine what is considered knowledge, how it is to be transmitted to new generations, and who will do the teaching. Legal and political institutions determine what laws regulate our lives, how and by whom they are enforced, and who will be prosecuted for which violations.

Institutions have great power to reward and penalize. They reward by providing career opportunities for some people and foreclosing them for others. They reward as well by the way social goods and services are distributed—by deciding who receives training and skills, medical care, formal education, political influence, moral support and self-respect, productive employment, fair treatment by the law, decent housing, self-confidence, and the promise of a secure future for self and children. No society will distribute social benefits in a perfectly equitable way. But no society need use race as a criterion to determine who will be rewarded and who punished. Any nation that permits race to affect the distribution of benefits from social policies is racist.

It is our thesis that institutional racism is deeply embedded in American society. Slavery was only the earliest and most blatant practice. Political, economic, educational, and religious policies cooperated with slaveholders to "keep the nigger in his place." Emancipation changed little. Jim Crow laws as well as residential and employment discrimination guaranteed that black citizens remained under the control of white citizens. Second-class citizenship quickly became a social fact as well as a legal status. Overt institutional racism was widely practiced throughout American society at least until World War II.

With desegregation in the armed forces and the passage of various civil rights bills, institutional racism no longer has the status of law. It is perpetuated nonetheless, sometimes by frightened and bigoted individuals, sometimes by good citizens merely carrying on "business as usual," and sometimes by well-intentioned but naive reformers. An attack on institutional racism is clearly the next task for Americans, white and black, who hope to obtain for their children a society less tense and more just than the one of the mid-1960's. It is no easy task. Individual, overt racist acts, such as the shotgun slaying of civil rights workers, are visible. Techniques of crime detection can be used to apprehend guilty parties, and, in theory, due process of law will punish them. To detect institutional racism, especially when it is unintentional or when it is disguised, is a very different task. And even when institutional racism is detected, it is seldom clear who is at fault. How can we say who is responsible for residential segregation, for poor education in ghetto schools, for extraordinarily high unemployment among black men, for racial stereotypes in history textbooks, for the concentration of political power in white society?

Our analysis begins with attention to ideological patterns in American society which historically and presently sustain practices appropriately labeled "institutionally racist." We then turn attention to the procedures of dominant American institutions: educational, economic, political, legal, and medical. It is as a result of practices within these institutions that black citizens in America are consistently penalized for reasons of color.

Quite obviously the social arrangements which fix unequal opportunities for black and white citizens can be traced back through American history—farther back, as a matter of fact, than even the beginning of slavery. Our purpose is not to rewrite American history, although that needs to be done. Rather our purpose in this initial chapter is to point out the historical roots of institutional racism by examining the ideology used to justify it. In understanding how deeply racist practices are embedded in the American experience and values, we can come to a fuller understanding of how contemporary social institutions have adapted to their heritage.

HISTORY AND IDEOLOGY

Some form of white supremacy, both as ideology and institutional arrangement, existed from the first day English immigrants, seeking freedom from religious intolerance, arrived on the North American continent. From the beginning, the early colonizers apparently considered themselves culturally superior to the natives they encountered. This sense of superiority over the Indians, which was fostered by the religious ideology they carried to the new land, found its expression in the self-proclaimed mission to civilize and Christianize—a mission which was to find its ultimate expression in ideas of a "manifest destiny" and a "white man's burden."

The early colonists were a deeply religious people. The church was the dominant social institution of their time, and the religious doctrines brought from England strongly influenced their contacts with the native Indians. The goals of the colonists were stated clearly:

> *Principal and Maine Ends* [of the Virginia colony] . . . were first to preach and baptize into *Christian Religion* and by propogation of the *Gospell*, to recover out of the arms of the *Divell*, a number of

poore and miserable soules, wrapt up unto death, in almost invinc-
ible ignorance . . . and to add our myte to the Treasury of
Heaven.[2]

Ignorance about the white man's God was sufficient proof in itself
of the inferiority of the Indian and, consequently, of the superiority
of the white civilization.

The mission impulse was doomed to failure. A shortage of mis-
sionaries and an unexpected resistance on the part of the Indian
(who was less sure that the white man's ways were inherently
superior) led to the dismantling of the few programs aimed at
Christianization. It became clear that conquering was, on balance,
less expensive and more efficient than "civilizing."

Thus began an extended process of genocide, giving rise to such
aphorisms as "The only good Indian is a dead Indian." It was at this
time that the ideology of white supremacy on the North American
continent took hold. Since Indians were capable of reaching only
the stage of "savage," they should not be allowed to impede the
forward (westward, to be exact) progress of white civilization. The
Church quickly acquiesced in this redefinition of the situation. The
disappearance of the nonwhite race in the path of expansionist
policies was widely interpreted as God's will. As one student of
America's history has written, "It apparently never seriously occurred to [spokesmen for Christianity] that where they saw the
mysterious law of God in the disappearance of the nonwhite races
before the advancing Anglo-Saxon, a disappearance which apparently occurred without anyone's willing it or doing anything to bring
it about, the actual process was a brutal one of oppression, dis-
possession, and even extermination."[3]

In short, what began as a movement to "civilize and Christianize"
the indigenous native population was converted into a racist force,
accompanied, as always, by a justificatory ideology. In retrospect,
the result is hardly surprising. The English colonists operated from
a premise which has continued to have a strong impact on American
thought: the Anglo-Saxon race is culturally and religiously superior;
neither the validity nor the integrity of alien cultures can be recog-

---

[2] Quoted in Thomas F. Gossett, *Race: The History of an Idea in America* (Dallas: SMU Press, 1963), p. 18.
[3] *Ibid.*, p. 196.

nized. (The Indian culture, though native to the land, was considered the alien one.) When it became clear that Indians could not be "saved," the settlers concluded that the race itself was inferior. This belief was strengthened by such racist theories as the Teutonic Theory of Origins, which pointed out the superiority of the Anglo-Saxons. The institution of slavery and its accompanying justification would seem to have been products of the same mentality.

It has, of course, been the white man's relationship with the black man which has led to the most powerful expressions of institutional racism in the society. This is a history which hardly needs retelling, although it might be instructive to consider how closely related was the justification of Indian extermination to that of black slavery. It was the heathenism or savagery, so-called, of the African, just as of the Indian, which became the early rationale for enslavement. A particularly ingenious version of the rationale is best known under the popular label "Social Darwinism."

The Social Darwinian theory of evolution greatly influenced social thought, hence social institutions, in nineteenth-century America. Social Darwinists extended the concept of biological evolution in the development of man to a concept of evolution in development of societies and civilizations. The nature of a society or nation or race was presumed to be the product of natural evolutionary forces. The evolutionary process was characterized by struggle and conflict in which the "stronger, more advanced, and more civilized" would naturally triumph over the "inferior, weaker, backward, and uncivilized" peoples.

> The idea of natural selection was translated to a struggle between individual members of a society; between members of classes of society, between different nations, and between different races. This conflict, far from being an evil thing, was nature's indispensable method of producing superior men, superior nations, and superior races.[4]

Such phrases as "the struggle for existence" and "the survival of the fittest" became *lingua franca,* and white Americans had a full-blown ideology to explain their treatment of the "inferior race."

The contemporary expression of Social Darwinian thinking is

[4] *Ibid.,* p. 145.

less blatant but essentially the same as the arguments used in the nineteenth century. The poverty and degradation of the nonwhite races in the United States are thought to be the result of an innate lack of ability rather than anything white society has done. Thus a long line of argument reaches its most recent expression in the now famous "Moynihan Report": the focal point of the race problem is to be found in the pathology of black society.

Social Darwinism was buttressed with two other ideas widely accepted in nineteenth-century America: manifest destiny and white man's burden. Briefly stated, manifest destiny was simply the idea that white Americans were destined, either by natural forces or by Divine Right, to control at least the North American continent and, in many versions of the theory, a much greater share of the earth's surface. Many churchmen supported the idea that such expansion was the will of God. The impact of this belief with respect to the Indians has already been noted. Let it suffice to say that manifest destiny helped provide the moral and theological justification for genocide. The belief that American expansion was a natural process was rooted in Social Darwinism. Expansionism was simply the natural growth process of a superior nation. This deterministic argument enjoyed wide popularity. Even those who were not comfortable with the overt racism of the expansionist argument were able to cooperate in policies of "liberation" in Cuba and the Philippines by emphasizing the evils of Spanish control. Many, however, felt no need to camouflage their racism. Albert J. Beveridge, Senator from Indiana, stated his position clearly:

> The American Republic is a part of the movement of a race—the most masterful race of history—and race movements are not to be stayed by the hand of man. They are mighty answers to Divine commands. Their leaders are not only statesmen of peoples—they are prophets of God. The inherent tendencies of a race are its highest law. They precede and survive all statutes, all constitutions. . . . The sovereign tendencies of our race are organization and government.[5]

In any case, if racism was not invoked as a justification for

[5] *Ibid.*, p. 318.

imperialist expansion in the first place, it subsequently became a justification for continued American control of the newly "acquired" territories. This was particularly true in the Philippines. "The control of one country by another and the denial of rights or citizenship to the Filipinos were difficult ideas to reconcile with the Declaration of Independence and with American institutions. In order to make these opposing ideas of government compatible at all, the proponents of the acquisition of the Philippines were forced to rely heavily on race theories." [6]

An argument commonly expressed was that the Filipinos were simply incapable of self-government. " 'The Declaration of Independence,' stated Beveridge, 'applies only to peoples capable of self-government. Otherwise, how dared we administer the affairs of the Indians? How dare we continue to govern them today?' " [7] The decision, therefore, as to who was capable of self-government and who was not so capable was left to the United States Government. The criteria were usually explicitly racist, as it was simply assumed that whites, at least Anglo-Saxons, had the "gift" of being able to govern themselves while the inferior nonwhite peoples were not so endowed.

The ideology of imperialist expansion had an easily foreseeable impact on the domestic race situation. As Ronald Segal points out in *The Race War,*

> Both North and South saw and accepted the implications. What was sauce for the Philippines, for Hawaii and Cuba, was sauce for the Southern Negro. If the stronger and cleverer race is free to impose its will upon "new-caught sullen peoples" on the other side of the globe, why not in South Carolina and Mississippi? asked the *Atlantic Monthly.* "No Republican leader," proclaimed Senator Tillman of South Carolina, ". . . will now dare to wave the bloody shirt and preach a crusade against the South's treatment of the Negro. The North has a bloody shirt of its own. Many thousands of them have been made into shrouds for murdered Filipinos, done to death because they were fighting for liberty." Throughout the United States doctrines of racial superiority received the assent of influential politi-

---

[6] *Ibid.,* p. 328.
[7] *Ibid.,* p. 329.

cians and noted academics. The very rationalizations that had eased the conscience of the slave trade now provided the sanction for imperial expansion.[8]

Another component of the ideology which has nurtured racist policies is that of "the white man's burden." This phrase comes from the title of a poem by Rudyard Kipling, which appeared in the United States in 1899. Whatever Kipling himself may have wished to convey, Americans soon popularized and adopted the concept as an encouragement for accepting the responsibility of looking after the affairs of the darker races. This notion of the "white man's burden" was that the white race, particularly Anglo-Saxons of Britain and America, should accept the (Christian) responsibility for helping the poor colored masses to find a better way of life.

It should be clear that this notion is no less racist than others previously mentioned. Behind the attitude lies the assumption of white supremacy. In exhorting Americans to follow British policy in this regard, the philosopher Josiah Royce stated the assumption clearly.

> . . . The Englishman, in his official and governmental dealings with backward peoples, has a great way of being superior without very often publicly saying that he is superior. You well know that in dealing, as an individual, with other individuals, trouble is seldom made by the fact that you are actually superior to another man in any respect. The trouble comes when you tell the other man, too stridently, that you are his superior. Be my superior, quietly, simply showing your superiority in your deeds, and very likely I shall love you for the very fact of your superiority. For we all love our leaders. But tell me I am your inferior, and then perhaps I may grow boyish, and may throw stones. Well, it is so with the races. Grant then that yours is the superior race. Then you can say little about the subject in your public dealings with the backward race. Superiority is best shown by good deeds and by few boasts.[9]

Both manifest destiny and the idea of a white man's burden, in disguised forms, continue to shape white America's values and policies. Manifest destiny has done much to stimulate the modern day

---

[8] Ronald Segal, *The Race War* (Baltimore: Penguin Books, 1967), p. 219.
[9] Gossett, p. 334.

myth that colored peoples are generally incapable of self-government. There are whites who continue to believe that black Afro-Americans are not ready to govern themselves. At best, blacks must first be "properly trained." Of course, this belief influences our relations with nonwhites in other areas of the world as well.

The authors have found the concept of manifest destiny helpful in analyzing white response to "black power." Black power is based on the belief that black people in America are capable of governing and controlling their own communities. White rejection of black power reflects, in part, the widely accepted white myth that blacks are incapable of self-government and must be controlled and governed by whites. Many whites apparently still share with Albert Beveridge the belief that "organization and government" are among the "sovereign tendencies of our race."

The belief in a "white man's burden" also has its modern-day counterpart, particularly in the attitudes and practices of so-called "white liberals" busily trying to solve "the Negro problem." The liberal often bears a strong sense of responsibility for helping the Negro find a better life. He generally characterizes the Negro as "disadvantaged," "unfortunate," or "culturally deprived." The liberal generally feels superior to the black man, although he is less likely to publicly state his sense of superiority. He may not even recognize his own racist sentiments. In any case, much like Josiah Royce, he senses that "superiority is best shown by good deeds and by few boasts." Liberal paternalism is reflected not only in individual attitudes but in the procedures and policies of institutions such as the welfare system and most "war on poverty" efforts.

It is obvious that recent reports and action plans carry on a traditional, if diversionary, view that has long been acceptable to most white Americans: that it is not white institutions but a few bigots plus the deprived status of Negroes that cause racial tension. Such a view is mythical. And the chapters to follow, as well as the special appendix prepared by Harold Baron, seek to free our thinking of such simple-minded explanations. We are not content with "explanations" of white-black relations that are apolitical, that would reduce the causes of racial tension to the level of psychological and personal factors. Three hundred years of American history cannot be encapsulated so easily. To ignore the network of institutional controls through which social benefits are allocated may be reassuring, but it is also bad social history. America is and has long been a racist nation, because it has and has long had a racist policy. This policy is not to be understood by listening to the proclamations of intent by leading citizens and government officials; nor is it to be understood by reading off a list of compensatory programs in business, education, and welfare. The policy can be understood only when we are willing to take a hard look at the continuing and irrefutable racist consequences of the major institutions in American life. The policy will be changed when we are willing to start the difficult task of remaking our institutions.

Chapter 2

Racial Practices in Economic Life

The United States has built the strongest, most productive economy known to man. The abundance is spread among not only the entrepreneurial class but also the laborers. It is safe to say that no people has ever enjoyed a standard of living as high as that found in white America. Yet black America remains bound in a poverty resembling that found in underdeveloped nations. The discrepancy between unprecedented white affluence and black poverty is the result of the almost total exclusion of black Americans from entrepreneurial activity and the market. The vast majority of blacks have functioned only as menial workers and exploited consumers. The present division of the economy along racial lines is the result of both intentional and unintentional institutional racism.

THE EXCLUSION OF BLACK PEOPLE
FROM FREE ENTERPRISE

Ownership of capital and the right to invest it in profit-making enterprises has always been associated with the American concept of freedom. Yet the white business world has consistently denied to black people the opportunity to control substantial financial resources. The total number of black-owned businesses in the United States is estimated at no more than 50,000. If black people owned businesses in proportion to their representation in the population, there would be ten times as many black businesses, or 500,000.[1] The discrepancy is actually greater than these figures indicate; many of the 50,000 enterprises listed as black-owned are proprietorships which can best be described as marginal in nature.

At the end of 1963, blacks owned or controlled only thirteen banks, fifty life insurance companies, and thirty-four federally insured savings and loan associations, with combined assets totaling $764 million or only 0.12 per cent of the total assets of financial institutions in the country.[2]

The National Association of Market Development, an association of businesses which serve predominantly black communities, has only 131 black-owned firms out of a total of 407 members.[3] The most startling fact of all is that the situation is deteriorating rather than improving. Between 1950 and 1960, the number of black businesses decreased by more than one-fifth of its original total.[4]

There are many problems within the ghetto itself which limit the development of black enterprise. The educational background of most black people effectively cripples them for highly skilled positions (see chapter on education). Years of experiencing white prejudice and personal failure have created a chasm of despair in the ghetto, which works against ambition and participation in business ventures. But major responsibility for the *de facto* racist situation continues to rest with the white business world.

The greatest difficulty the black would-be businessman faces is the lack of available credit. Aside from overt discrimination among financiers, the black entrepreneur is at a sharp disadvantage in the face of credit standards designed to measure the reliability of white applicants. A financial institution considering a loan application examines the credit history of the applicant, the collateral to be held against the loan, the prospects for business success, and other related criteria. The black man is more likely than the white man to

---

[1] "The Ordeal of the Black Businessman," *Newsweek*, March 4, 1968, p. 72.

[2] Andrew Brimmer, "The Negro in the National Economy," in *The American Negro Reference Book*, ed. John P. David (Englewood Cliffs, N.J.: Prentice-Hall, Inc., 1966), p. 297.

[3] *Ibid.*, pp. 290–91.

[4] *Ibid.*, p. 295.

have a poor credit record due to the loan sharks and exploitative merchants that feed off ghetto residents. Black people usually have no property or investments that could be used as collateral. And finally, the black businessman who wishes to locate in his own community, where the income level is at or near the poverty line, will have poorer prospects for success than the white merchant in the white middle-class community. *The present standards, when applied without regard to race, will lead to more white ownership of enterprises and less black participation in the economy.*

There are strong indications that the standards for assessing credit risk are not good measures of a black man's reliability. During the years 1954–1963, the Federal Small Business Administration made a total of 432 loans. Of this number only seven loans went to black businesses despite the fact that the organization was ostensibly following nondiscriminatory policies.[5] Then, in 1964, the Small Business Administration launched its 6 × 6 plan: $6,000 for six years. The SBA evaluated applicants for this program on criteria other than credit history or collateral. Of 219 loans made, 98 went to black people. Only eight of the 219 were delinquent and none were liquidated. These statistics cast doubt on the idea that black businesses are a high credit risk.

The black businessman is also plagued by insurance costs which are as much as three times higher than those that most whites pay. Insurance companies are hesitant to cover ghetto property due to the danger of possible damage in civil disturbances; only very high premiums will draw them back into the black community.

Black entrepreneurs, along with other small businessmen in the nation, face growing pressure from the large corporations that increasingly dominate the economy. The trend is symbolized by the disappearance of the corner grocery store and the proliferation of chain supermarkets. The "little man" will eventually disappear from the American business scene if conditions do not change in some unforeseen way. The efficient corporate giants already control major segments of both the retail and industrial sectors of the economy. This development can only mean less black participation in business

---

[5] Eugene Foley, "The Negro Businessman: In Search of a Tradition," in *The Negro American,* ed. T. Parsons and K. B. Clark (Boston: Beacon Press, 1966), p. 575.

since there is virtually no black representation at the level of national corporation management.

The fact is that the lack of black-owned businesses reinforces the dependency of black people upon the economic interests of the white economic community. White businesses share in the responsibility to dissolve this relationship of economic dependency. Although small in magnitude, the SBA's 6 × 6 plan, mentioned above, is a step in this direction. Such programs represent a significant start in that they lay the groundwork for bigger, more inclusive programs. After the recent rebellions, New York began the nation's first mandatory high-risk pool to provide insurance for businessmen in the ghetto. The bill provides for a joint underwriting fund to share losses among the leading insurance companies. Programs like this will hopefully make insurance for black economic ventures cheaper and easier to obtain. Philadelphia's First Banking and Trust Company agreed in September of 1966 to funnel loans into the ghetto through an all-black organization. Steps are being taken, but they are not coordinated, planned, or really encouraged.

Of primary importance is the supplying of financial resources to the black community. The SBA has shown that loans to blacks can be safe and profitable. The organization of new black banks would be instrumental in persuading other financial organizations to invest in the ghetto. The competition from the black-owned banks would make the other institutions more sensitive to the needs of black customers. There is evidence for this, especially in Atlanta, Georgia, and Durham, North Carolina.

There are other steps that private enterprise and the government could take. Chain stores or industries could franchise black-owned and operated units within the ghettos. This type of endeavor speaks directly to the deprivation of the ghetto, which is lack of capital power. Such a project was developed in south-central Los Angeles by Aerojet General, a West Coast subsidiary of General Tire and Rubber Company. Aerojet General has invested $1,333,000 to set up an independent, black-run plant. Also, there are other construction programs which could be offered to black contractors: FHA's 3 per cent insured loans for low-income housing developments, the new two-thirds grant program for small public facilities, and public housing units.

It should be kept in mind that economic assistance of any form should not be imposed on the black community without its consent, nor should whites follow any preference for one economic form over another in giving financial aid to the ghettos. Much of the above discussion could be misconstrued as a defense of "black capitalism." It is probable that many black communities across the nation will decide to use the model of private entrepreneurial activity as a means to the end of economic security. But it is also quite possible that groups of black people will lead the way in the development of new cooperative and community-owned forms of production and marketing. Financial resources should be made available for these experiments, and not just to "safe" black businessmen who have adopted all the mores and values of the dominant white economic system.

THE BLACK WORKER

The black population of the United States has not only been excluded from the business world, but it has also been relegated to the lowest level of the laboring class. Although token efforts have been made to hire and promote blacks to a greater extent during the last decade, there has been no measurable improvement in the status of the black worker relative to the general population.

The lack of high-income, skilled jobs among black workers largely accounts for the fact that black median family income was only 58 per cent of white median income in 1966.[6] It is even more discouraging to note that the purchasing power of the black family relative to the white family has declined over the past twenty years. In constant 1965 dollars, median nonwhite family income in 1947 was $2,174 lower than median white income. By 1966, the gap had grown to $3,036.[7]

The subordinate economic status of black workers can be traced to unemployment and underemployment. Black unemployment has

---

[6] *Report of the National Advisory Commission on Civil Disorders* (New York: Bantam Books, 1968), p. 251.
[7] *Ibid.*, p. 251.

remained throughout the postwar period at a rate double that for whites. Since 1954, despite the unprecedented period of sustained economic growth, the black unemployment rate has been continuously above the 6 per cent "recession" level which is used as a signal of serious economic difficulties when it is prevalent for the entire work force.[8]

More serious than unemployment is the vast amount of *underemployment*. The Riot Commission reports (using 1966 data) that if nonwhite employment were upgraded proportionately to the level of white employment, about $4.8 billion in additional income would be produced. This is significantly greater than the $1.5 billion in additional income that would be gained if nonwhite unemployment were to be reduced to the level of white unemployment.[9]

Behind these figures lies a record of overt racial discrimination in hiring and promotions that persists into the present. Firms have refused to hire black people or they have assigned black workers to menial positions below their capabilities. Discriminatory practices have persisted through the civil rights era despite government actions and the proclamations of concern by business leaders. Commenting about the disparity in wage levels, the Kerner Commission states, "However, the differentials are so large and so universal at all educational levels that they clearly reflect the patterns of discrimination which characterize hiring and promotion practices in many segments of the economy."[10]

Beyond blatant racism, there are a variety of structural factors that are working against black workers who already occupy the bottom of the economic ladder. In the past the American economy successfully absorbed huge masses of unskilled laborers. But the postwar urban scene into which black people have moved is very different from nineteenth-century America, which found room for the European immigrant groups. The demand for unskilled labor was much greater in the last century and the early part of the twentieth than it is now. The steady advance of automation has raised the skill-level required to obtain steady employment. Further-

[8] *Ibid.*, p. 253.
[9] *Ibid.*, p. 255.
[10] *Ibid.*, p. 256.

more, no American institution has taken sufficient steps to insure that black people gain the skills necessary for entry into the modern job market.

Industry once flourished in the central cities, but much of it in recent decades has followed the pattern of white emigration to the suburbs. The "white flight" to the suburbs is itself motivated by prejudice and myths about falling property values. That business and industry would follow the "money, management, and workers" out of the city is not surprising. But the ghetto resident is left without the means to reach most jobs. Many metropolitan centers are woefully deficient in providing low-cost public transportation between outlying industries and the inner city.

The soaring technological economy and the job opportunities for blacks are drawing farther apart rather than closer. To stem this growing gap, businessmen of a liberal cast talk now of the business world taking a backward step in an effort to draw the black community along. But this plan asks business to behave in an unbusinesslike way, something it has rarely been known to do. The fundamental rule by which all American enterprises live is to make a profit. A business that does not earn a profit is not a business very long. Managers seek the lowest possible production costs and maximum efficiency. Therefore, personnel are hired according to their productivity and efficiency. The average white man will be much more likely to have the training, references, and cultural background needed to convince an employer that he will contribute to the productivity and efficiency of the business. Often a firm will use a written test to assist in rating applicants. These tests are almost always designed to test ability in the context of white society, and therefore they discriminate against black people, as do IQ and aptitude tests in public schools (see Chap. 3, pp. 35–37).

Interviews are used by employers to gauge the personality of a prospective worker. Especially in white collar positions, the ability of an individual to fit into the operation without causing psychological disruption among the other workers is a crucial factor in the evaluation. The applicant should conform to accepted standards of dress, speech, and manners. The employer evaluates the job-seeker from the ghetto by means of a code of appearance and behavior that is very different from that which is considered acceptable in the black community. Too often a black person must act "white" in order to obtain a job, although his ability to conform to white culture may have little to do with whether he can perform the task for which he is hired. The black worker faces the same battery of problems with respect to promotion that he did when he originally sought employment. In addition, in many cases the worker will lose all seniority if he accepts a promotion. One study indicates that black workers more often than whites will choose to retain their seniority rather than accept promotion.[11] This behavior reflects the understanding of the black worker that if he should lose his job it is much more difficult for him to find new employment than for a white man to relocate.

The attitudes and policies of management are not the only source of racial discrimination in the job market. Labor unions have closed themselves tightly in the face of the black request for more and better jobs. The black people arrived on the urban scene after the unions had solidified into strong power groups. Consequently they were not able to join hands with other segments of the labor force as the great waves of European immigrants had done in previous decades. Now the labor unions are agencies that protect their mostly white membership from potential workers, many of whom are black. Unions are an obstacle for black people rather than an institutional channel by which they can gain access to American affluence.

The AFL–CIO and other national labor organizations have stated their opposition to racial discrimination over and over again during the past two decades, yet the good intentions have not penetrated to the level of the union locals. A. Philip Randolph, president of the Brotherhood of Sleeping Car Porters, stated in 1962 that black workers are discriminated against "in apprenticeship training, hiring policies, seniority lists, pay scales, and job assignments in many locals, especially the building trades." [12] The statistics show that

---

[11] James R. Wetzel and Susan Holland, "Poverty Areas of Our Major Cities," *Monthly Labor Review*, 89, October 1966, 1105–10.
[12] Labor Research Association, *Labor Fact Book* (New York: International Publishers, 1963), p. 83.
[13] *Ibid.*, p. 83.

Randolph was correct. In 1962, out of a labor force of 10.5 million black workers, only 1.5 million were members of trade unions.[13] The refusal to admit black men to union apprenticeship programs has done much to create this inequity. Both the NAACP and the U.S. Civil Rights Commission in the early 1960's attacked the problem of discrimination in apprenticeships. The commission investigation produced some detailed examples within trade unions:

a. In St. Louis, out of 1,667 apprentices in craft programs in the building, metals, and printing trades, only seven were black.
b. In Atlanta, the construction industry had twenty black apprentices out of a total of 700 positions. All of the blacks were in the dirtier trowel trades—bricklaying, plastering, lathing, and cement finishing.
c. In Baltimore, out of 750 building trade apprentices, only twenty were black.
d. In both Atlanta and Baltimore, there were no black apprentices in the Iron Workers, the Plumbers, the Brotherhood of Electrical Workers, the Sheet and Metal Workers, and the Painters Union.
e. In Detroit less than 2 per cent of all craft union apprentices were black.[14]

The situation within the giant industrial unions such as the UAW is slightly different. General union membership is easy to obtain for those black people in unskilled assembly-line positions. However, the apprenticeships that could lead to higher paying, skilled positions are for the most part reserved for whites. For example, one Detroit manufacturing company had a labor force that was 23 per cent black; but out of 289 apprenticeships, only one was held by a black man. In a joint apprenticeship program of the UAW and the Automotive Tool and Die Makers Association in Detroit, one out of 370 positions was occupied by a black man.[15]

[14] Arthur Roos and Herbert Hill, *Employment, Race and Poverty* (New York: Harcourt, Brace & World, Inc., 1967), p. 409.
[15] *Ibid.*, p. 410.

Labor organizations responded to the charges of the NAACP and Civil Rights Commission by pointing to the removal of discriminatory clauses from their constitutions, but racist policies remain unmitigated at the local level. There have also been a few attempts to integrate the union hierarchy, but these have amounted to little more than token efforts. For example, that George M. Harrison, president of the Brotherhood of Railway and Steamship Clerks, is a member of the Civil Rights Committee of the AFL–CIO while his own union has discriminated against blacks indicates the type of effort being taken by labor unions to offer equal opportunity to blacks.[16] This form of noncompliance with directives from the central office of the AFL–CIO is rampant, and it is a clear indication that the labor movement is in a poor position to uphold and respect its own policies.

No effective pressure to change discriminatory practices has been brought to bear on the unions from outside. Labor leaders voice the rhetoric of integration, but they have not found an effective way of changing grass-roots attitudes. The federal government has barely begun to grapple with the problem. The National Labor Relations Board, which is constituted totally of white men, has been ineffective. The Department of Labor has been unable to enforce Sec. 703(d) of the 1964 Civil Rights Act, which forbids discrimination in apprenticeship programs. In Philadelphia, for example, not one of the four important craft unions in the building trades has a program that meets the legal regulations of the Bureau of Apprenticeship and Training.

It will be surprising if government agencies seriously attack union racism, for the labor force constitutes a powerful portion of the electorate, which can destroy an administration that does not meet the favor of the workers. A campaign to eradicate grass-roots union racism, if it had any substance at all, would probably signal the end of many political careers. It is interesting to note that although the President's Commission on Civil Disorders contains a relatively thorough discussion of racist business practices, it includes only *one* sentence referring to union discrimination.

---

[16] *Labor Fact Book,* p. 83.

THE EXPLOITED BLACK CONSUMER

The black person who is fortunate enough to be employed has not yet achieved the financial security of the white wage earner. The black urban communities are filled with stores and businesses that are geared to extract the maximum profit from a clientele that is trapped in the ghetto by prejudice and poor public transportation. Most of these stores are owned by white merchants, so the proceeds return to the white community rather than staying in the ghetto where they are needed.

Ghetto residents pay more for all kinds of goods and services than do people living in white neighborhoods. According to testimony by Paul Rand Dixon, chairman of the FTC, an item selling wholesale at $100 would retail on the average for $165 in a general merchandise store and for $250 in a low-income specialty store.[17] Thus the customers of these outlets are paying a premium of about 52 per cent.

Television, radio, billboards and other advertising media constantly encourage black Americans to acquire the symbols of the affluent society. Since good housing is difficult for black people to find or to finance, they invest in less expensive, durable goods such as cars, stereo sets, televisions, and clothing. These items would be beyond the reach of most black wage earners if it were not for the ghetto merchants who conveniently extend credit to anyone, at exorbitant rates.

All the states require by law that installment contracts state specifically how much the buyer is paying for credit. But a study made by David Caplovitz in New York demonstrated that many merchants in low-income areas ignore installment contracts altogether, or if they do use them, the merchants intentionally do not differentiate between the cost of credit and the cost of the product. Merchants often emphasize the small down payment and the low monthly installments without informing the buyer about the length of the contract. The ghetto businessman compensates for extending

---

[17] *Advisory Commission on Civil Disorders*, p. 276.

credit to high-risk buyers by selling inferior merchandise whose price has been marked up 200 to 300 per cent.[18]

The local merchants are not the only parties guilty of consumer exploitation. Many of the unscrupulous practices could not exist were it not for the finance companies and banks that buy up unpaid installment contracts from merchants. These institutions know by the very terms and form of the contract that they are purchasing dishonest and exploitative contracts, yet they continue to do so.

Frequently merchants will not place price tags on items in ghetto stores. This practice allows the salesman to gauge the naiveté of the customer and consequently how much he can charge without causing suspicion.[19]

Perhaps the most serious form of consumer exploitation directed at black people is found in the housing market. Realtors, government housing agencies, and financial institutions have together managed to create almost total residential separation of the races. The black family that has accumulated sufficient resources has great difficulty purchasing or renting a house in a white community. Available housing in the ghetto tends to be overpriced and suffering from inadequate maintenance. The Kerner Commission reported that, based on a study of Newark, New Jersey, "nonwhites were paying a definite 'color tax' of apparently well over 10 per cent on housing. *This condition prevails in most racial ghettos.*"[20]

Real estate agencies play the largest role in maintaining segregated communities. The Washington lobby of the National Association of Real Estate Boards testified against the acceptance of the fair housing provision of the 1966 civil rights bill. The association represents 83,000 realtors in every state of the Union. If the national organization is so blatant in its opposition to fair housing, it can be imagined how local agencies operate.[21]

A common realty practice is known as "blockbusting." In this

---

[18] David Caplovitz, *The Poor Pay More* (New York: The Free Press of Glencoe, 1967), Chaps. 2 & 6.

[19] *Ibid.*, p. 17.

[20] *Advisory Commission on Civil Disorders*, p. 252. (Italics added.)

[21] Hearings Before Subcommittee No. 5 of the Committee on the Judiciary, House of Representatives, 89th Congress, Second Session, "Statement of Alan L. Emlen, Chairman, Realtor's Washington Committee, National Association of Real Estate Boards," pp. 1585–1603.

operation, the realtor persuades a black family to move into an all-white neighborhood. The realtor then does everything in his power to foster anxiety over falling property prices among the white home-owners. The agent then capitalizes on the psychological insecurity of the whites by buying their homes at prices below market value and then reselling the property at a handsome profit to minority families. A Philadelphia study by two real estate economists, Chester Rapkin and William G. Gimby, revealed the profitability of such speculative activities. On the average, blockbusters double their investment in less than two years.[22]

The blockbusting racket is based on a myth, according to an urban sociologist, Sherwood Ross, and economist Luigi Laurenti. A study of over 1.3 million homes in forty-seven major cities led to the con-clusion that property values do not decline when black families move into a neighborhood. The authors state: "White homeowners talked into selling short by crooked real estate swindlers and panic-peddlers would find their homes rising steadily in value if they would only hold on to them." [23] Laurenti, who studied one thousand integrated neighborhoods, found that prices rose in 44 per cent of the cases when blacks entered, remained stable in 41 per cent, and declined in only 15 per cent relative to closely matched white neighborhoods.[24]

Federal housing programs have also contributed to racial separa-tion and inadequate housing for black people. The Federal Housing Administration from its inception in 1934 has favored racially homogeneous neighborhoods. The FHA manual stated: "If a neighborhood is to retain stability, it is necessary that properties shall continue to be occupied by the same society and race group." The FHA sometimes refused altogether to provide mortgage insur-ance for integrated housing. More often, it employed delaying tactics which effectively stalled such projects until they failed financially or accepted segregation. After the Supreme Court in

[22] George Grier, *Equality and Beyond* (Chicago: Quadrangle Books, 1966), p. 35.
[23] Hearings Before Subcommittee No. 5 of the Committee on the Judi-ciary, House of Representatives, 89th Congress, Second Session, Statement by Attorney General Katzenbach, Exhibit No. 6, pp. 1228–30, No. 6, pp. 1219–24.
[24] Grier, p. 34.

1948 ruled against racially restrictive covenants in housing codes, the FHA dropped the discriminatory phrases in its charter but continued to insure mortgages with restrictive covenants.

Not only has the FHA historically supported segregation as financially sound policy, but it has established credit requirement for housing loans that discriminate against the black populace. FHA requires a minimum present income, good prospects for future income, and evidence of faithful repayment of past obligations. It has been shown earlier that black people are systematically excluded by criteria of this nature due to their position at the bottom of the economy. The result has been that although the FHA loan program has become the backbone of white suburban housing, it has not appreciably changed the housing situation for black people.

The massive urban renewal programs of recent years were designed to eliminate much slum housing and thereby beautify the core section of the major cities. But most slums have been replaced with public facilities and high-income housing. The black people that are evicted by the bulldozers cannot return to live in the area, but must seek out other areas of low-rent housing. Urban renewal may beautify the cities, but it *adds* to the housing problems of minority citizens.

In addition to real estate interests and federal housing programs, the credit institutions of the country share the responsibility for segregated housing. Banks, savings and loan associations, and insurance companies finance 70 per cent of all mortgages. They invest where they believe the risk is least and the property is most marketable. Investment directors continue to regard areas that are becoming integrated as poor risks despite studies which indicate that prices remain stable or rise in most integrated communities. Moreover, investors continue to display a racial bias that regards black people even with the proper credentials as poorer credit risks than whites.

The difficulty of obtaining loans from established firms means that many black people are forced to deal with independent speculators. This type of arrangement usually entails interest rates of 19 per cent or more, and families can be dispossessed after five days for failure to make a payment (by comparison, the FHA interest rate is between 5 and 7 per cent).

In recent years a number of laws have been passed at the federal level that are aimed at stopping racial discrimination in housing. A Supreme Court decision of 1968 extends the concept of open housing to all forms of residence including simple family dwelling. But laws can do very little to correct an injustice that is rooted deeply in the nation's economic pattern. Open housing laws, despite their intent, are limited in beneficial impact since they must be superimposed on a housing market and housing programs which are racist in their structure. Given the present structure and method of federal intervention in the area of housing, even complete nondiscrimination in regard to federal benefits would not greatly affect the continuing expansion of segregated patterns of residence. Residential segregation is a fact in this country. It will persist until there is massive action for its curtailment. Financial institutions must be willing to extend credit to many more minority applicants. If necessary, the federal government can insure their loans. The conservative life insurance industry has committed itself to a profitable investment of $1 billion of its $17 billion in the ghettos. This is a step in the right direction. The Rent Supplement Act, which provides federal rent subsidies to low-income families, is also a step. But each of these programs just cures the symptoms; they do not reach the disease. To solve the housing problem, a stop must be put to all economic forces which perpetuate residential segregation. Realtors must be forced to change their ways. Mortgages must be made easier to get. But, above all, jobs and black credit institutions must be made accessible to the un- and under-employed in the ghetto so that the normal avenues of institutional financing are open to them.

Ending the exploitative system of black economic dependence will be a task of overwhelming magnitude. There is no single answer to the three-fold oppression described in this section. Even a massive job program only touches at a single issue of secondary importance; if all black unemployment were wiped out, the problems of underemployment, lack of black capital, and consumer exploitation would persist.

Many of the issues cannot be touched by legislation. Laws cannot change credit criteria in a way that will allow large amounts of capital to flow into black hands nor can legal action force unions to admit black laborers. Progress will be made only as the black com-

munity organizes to exert pressure on white structures and as white
people become aware that major sacrifices must be made at all
levels. To right the wrongs of the past will be a long and costly
process involving profound changes in the definition of self-interest
for the American economy.

The critical issue is control. Reforms in the areas of employment,
union practices, consumer exploitation and ownership, and so forth
promote effective change only insofar as they enable black people to
move toward control of substantial economic resources. Only then
will it be possible for blacks to end their dependency on white
America and to develop economic institutions to meet their needs.

Chapter 3

The Subeducation of Black Children

Along with numerous other official and semiofficial documents, the Kerner Commission Report describes the failure of American education: ". . . for the many minorities and particularly for the children of the racial ghetto, the schools have failed to provide the educational experience which could help overcome the effects of discrimination and deprivation." [1] And, just as the many other reports, the Kerner Report stresses that more resources are needed—higher pay for teachers, improved teaching materials, newer and better maintained buildings, and so forth. Although expenditure per pupil tends to be much lower in the inner-city schools than the suburban school, grants-in-aid to city schools cannot alone solve the educational crisis.

White liberals have long failed to distinguish between resources and control of resources. Reform group after reform group speaks of spending more money but remains silent about sharing power. But much of what ails the inner-city school can be traced to one overriding fact: the people who are making decisions about what and how black children are to be taught, and how their progress is to be evaluated, have little understanding of black people and their culture. There are too few black teachers, and black principals and superintendents remain exceedingly rare. The unification of school districts has increased the distance between centralized boards of administrators and the local community. Although the trend toward

[1] *Report of the National Advisory Commission on Civil Disorders* (New York: Bantam Books, 1968), p. 425.

31

larger districts increases the efficiency of school administration in some respects, this trend usually decreases administrative responsiveness to the community in such important policy areas as hiring and curriculum. This is most evident when unification joins a majority of white schools with a smaller number of black schools. The district administration tends more often than not to reflect the needs of the white students at the expense of the less well understood needs of the black children. The same logic explains why so many black leaders are cool toward programs designed to eliminate local, segregated schools by bussing black or black and white children to large educational centers. While many educators feel that these centers could bring both integration and higher educational standards, the centers could give black people even less control over their children's education. The integration would still be on a white-controlled basis.

As a consequence of centralization of power in white hands, most ghetto schools confront black children with a curriculum and a set of learning conditions which do not relate to the students' life outside school. Textbooks and procedures are developed by and for whites and have little relevance to black parents with a Southern, rural background, or their ghetto-raised children. Even where "Negro history" is offered, it is still the white authorities who decide which black people are worth discussing. And it is the white authorities who pick the teachers to teach "Negro history." "From the classroom to the PTA, [black children] discover that the school does not like them, does not respond to them, does not appreciate their culture, and does not think they can learn." [2]

The parents and the leaders of the black community who recognize the problems of the schools are effectively cut off from any power to make changes in the education of their children. Hess and Shipman found that "working class [black] mothers feel a powerlessness and a lack of personal effectiveness against the authority of the school system, although they have great respect for education as an important tool for achieving a better status in life." [3]

[2] Frank Riessman, "The Culturally Deprived Child: A New View," U.S. Office of Education (1963), p. 8.
[3] Robert D. Hess and Virginia Shipman, "Maternal Attitude Toward the School and the Role of the Pupil: Some Social Class Comparisons" (Unpublished manuscript), p. 21.

And Dr. Pearl states: "The more deprived the background of the child, the less power he has in our educational system."[4] Black people are understandably alienated from a school system which refuses to recognize them.

School authorities often rationalize the hostility evident in dropout rates, absenteeism, discipline problems, and complaints by teachers of lack of parental concern by saying that poor people, "culturally deprived people," or "the disadvantaged" do not value education. This is a fallacious argument that conveniently shifts the blame. A study by Hall and Shipman on the attitudes of black mothers demonstrated that 73 per cent of their subjects who came from the lowest socioeconomic group wanted their children to attend college. Another study shows that in every socioeconomic class black parents have higher educational and occupational aspirations for their children than white people.[5] *The problem is not a lack of interest in education, but a lack of power.*

As the situation now stands, the white "experts" in the educational system tend to view black students as potential whites with little consideration given to their distinct culture and style of life. Our educators have insisted, consciously or unconsciously, that black children be educated out of their blackness.

A specialist in urban education illustrates the typical approach in defining the problem as "how to educate the inner-city child out of his subculture into society's mainstream . . . while preserving and developing personal elements of individuality and divergency, as well as the positive elements of his culture."[6] Such an approach demands that blacks recognize "society's mainstream" (white) as good, and the "inner-city subculture" (black and other minority ethnic groups) as bad. James Farmer, Assistant Secretary of HEW, has clarified the psychological implications for black people:

[4] Arthur Pearl, *Educational Change: Why—How—For Whom* (compiled from his speeches by the San Francisco Human Rights Commission), p. 6.

[5] Martin Deutsch and Bert Brown, "Social Influences in Negro and White Intelligence Differences," *Journal of Social Issues,* 20, No. 2 (April 1964), p. 312.

[6] A. Harry Passow, "Instructional Content for Depressed Urban Centers: Problems and Approaches" in *Education of the Disadvantaged,* A. Harry Passow and others, editors (New York: Holt, Rinehart, & Winston, 1967), p. 352.

America would only become colorblind when we gave up our color. The white man, who presumably has no color, would have to give up only his prejudices. We would have to give up our identities. Thus, we would usher in the Great Day with an act of complete self-denial and self-abasement. We would achieve equality by conceding racism's charge: that our skins were an affliction; that our history is one long humiliation; that we are empty of distinctive traditions and any legitimate source of pride.[7]

Social scientists and educators attempt to describe and explain educational difficulties of black pupils solely on the basis of "lower socioeconomic class" or "low status group." This approach obscures the relationship between race and membership in low socioeconomic groups. Socioeconomic status is a reliable base for predicting the level of educational achievement, but it considers black and white pupils from the same perspective, ignoring the effects of individual and institutional racism on black children and ignoring cultural differences in determining curriculum. The definition of the problem in terms of economics and status, to the exclusion of racial and cultural factors, leads educators to seek to bring the "inner-city child" out of his subculture rather than to change the structure of the educational system so that schools will recognize, accept, and respond to the different culture and to learn to teach children successfully within it.

Within the present educational apparatus, black students suffer from institutionalized discrimination in many ways but particularly in IQ testing, classroom ability grouping, and negative teacher attitudes. The combined effect of these factors is a progressive lessening of the child's self-esteem as he proceeds through school. Further, within each socioeconomic group the self-esteem of black children is less than that of white children. The self-concepts of black children of the ghetto, who bear the double stigma of blackness and poverty, are consistently lowest of all. The result of this process is a steady decline in academic performance, particularly in the critical skills of verbal and reading ability. "In the metropolitan Northeast Negro students on the average begin the first

[7] James Farmer, as quoted by Charles Farber in *White Reflections on Black Power* (Grand Rapids, Mich.: William B. Eerdmans Publishing Co., 1967), p. 22.

grade with somewhat lower scores on standard achievement tests than white, are about 1.6 grades behind white students by the sixth grade and have fallen 3.3 grades behind white students by the twelfth grade." [8] IQ scores of ghetto black children decline as they progress through school instead of increasing with age, as does a child's IQ score under normal conditions.

IQ TESTING

Among experts in the field of IQ testing, there is considerable agreement that environment, not innate intelligence, is responsible for performance on IQ and school placement tests. Professor Sexton in *Education and Income* writes, "there is not a shred of proof that the IQ tests are valid measures of native intelligence, and in fact there is much proof that they are not." [9] Concerning the use of intelligence tests, Dr. Leonard Kornberg states: "we have worked with a narrow view of a general ability of intelligence—one these children ("culturally disadvantaged") always seemed to lack, one that sometimes seemed to be a middle-class invention." [10] "An only daughter of well-to-do white city dwellers shows up best of all. Small wonder since the tests are made up by well-to-do, white, city dwellers and favor their vocabulary." [11] IQ tests discriminate against low-income groups. Children from higher income families more often live in the cultural environments that produce superior test performance.

IQ tests discriminate racially as well as against low socioeconomic status. Differences in scores between socioeconomic classes are not as marked among black children as among whites, and in every socioeconomic group black children score lower than their white counterparts. This is due partly to the overall effects of institutional

[8] U.S. Department of Health, Education, and Welfare, *Equality of Educational Opportunity* (Coleman Report), 1966, p. 20.
[9] Patricia Sexton, *Education and Income* (New York: Viking Press, 1961), p. 40.
[10] L. Kornberg, "Meaningful Teachers for Alienated Children," in *Education in Depressed Areas* (New York: Teachers College, Columbia University, 1963), p. 275.
[11] Sexton, p. 48.

racism and partly to cultural differences. The white family has a greater opportunity to live in an area where children will be exposed to the kind of environment that will produce good results on the tests, regardless of the socioeconomic status of the family. Martin Deutsch and Bert Brown conclude: "the social class gradations are less marked for the Negroes because Negro life in a caste society is considerably more homogeneous than is life for the majority group. This makes it extremely difficult ever to really match racial groups meaningfully on class status as the context and history of social experience are so different." [12]

There are cultural differences between the average black and the average white regardless of socioeconomic level. The IQ tests are centered around the typically white middle-class way of life. Black people on the whole have different tastes and a different vocabulary and different experiences from white people. These cultural differences are not accounted for in tests written by whites. It is highly probable that on a ghetto-culture-oriented IQ test, whites would as consistently score below blacks as black score below whites on our present tests.

The so-called culture-free tests recently devised are inherently contradictory. Their form and language and the conditions under which they are given cannot fail to be products of a culture. For example, the race of the person who administers the exam influences the results. In fact, the very practice of using a pencil and paper test to measure intelligence is itself a factor that will culturally bias the examination.

The testing process, if it is to work for educational improvement in ghetto schools, must be placed under the aegis of black educators who can work with the local community. At this stage in history, only a black man who has grown up within the racial ghetto can develop tests and testing processes which will give an accurate assessment of a black student's basic talents. In many cases, the black community may wish to abolish all IQ testing until such times as there may be a new definition of innate intelligence as opposed to environmental influences.

---

[12] Deutsch and Brown, p. 26.

There is much evidence that in a situation of poverty and oppression, any type of test for innate intelligence is misleading. Israeli educators were faced with immigrant children from North Africa and the Middle East who, like our ghetto children, scored lower than other youngsters at the start of school and fell progressively further behind as the years went along. These educators were not bound by prejudice and did not assume "slowness" to be the cause. They were able to evaluate the problem as "an impoverished environment . . . a lack of stimulation, particularly of a verbal sort in the early years." [13] And these educators were able to correct the disadvantages.

In spite of the evidence indicating that present IQ tests are economically, racially, and culturally biased, IQ scores are usually the basis for a child's placement into an ability group. The test results strongly influence the teacher's attitudes toward the student. Consequently, a student's scores largely determine the quality of education he will receive, an education which in turn continues to affect his test performance.

ABILITY GROUPING

Grouping students within a school according to their ability is not a new practice in American education, but it has taken on a new use and greater significance since the Supreme Court decision of 1954. Ability groups now often serve to maintain segregated classrooms in "desegregated" schools. Since test scores and earlier levels of achievement are used for placement in ability groups, black children are more often placed in the lower groups. The St. Louis pattern is common: "a disproportionate percentage of students in track I (the highest track) have been white and a similar disproportion in track III (lowest) have been Negro." [14]

[13] Charles E. Silberman, *Crisis in Black and White* (New York: Random House, 1964), p. 276.
[14] U.S. Civil Rights Commission, *Civil Rights U.S.A., Public Schools, Cities in the North and West* (Washington, D.C.: Government Printing Office, 1962), p. 292.

St. Louis has two special tracks. A super-track with an intensive college-prep curriculum is presently limited to three high schools, one with 30 per cent Negro enrollment and two which are essentially all-white. A disproportionately small percentage of black students attend high school where the super-track is available, and black exclusion is rendered yet more complete by the criteria for placement in this track: IQ test scores above 130, supported by superior achievement in the first four grades. The result is that only 5 to 10 per cent of the students in this "gifted child" program are black. The other special track is for the "retarded student." Since the basis for retardation is an IQ score below 80, the black youngster is once again cheated by the use of the IQ tests. He is far more likely to be branded "retarded" and thus to be taught a limited curriculum. Seventy-five per cent of the "retarded" elementary school students and 50 per cent of the "terminal" high school students are black. The high school percentage is lower because so many black students drop out when they reach the legal age.[15]

The tracking system also can become the tool of prejudiced school administrators. Nathaniel Hicherson, Director of Education, Anti-Defamation League, Los Angeles, states that racial minorities "are discriminated against by bigoted and race-minded school officials. They are channeled out of academic courses by counselors who have not one bit of training for dealing with minority group children. They are evaluated as slow learners and herded into slow learning groups as early as the first grade on the basis of observation by teachers who themselves may be filled with prejudice or sympathy for the 'poor little things.' "[16]

Whatever the basis for placement, the tracking system discriminates against black children. In Washington, D.C., a federal court abolished tracking as unconstitutional and discriminatory: "Tracking condemned black and poor children, on the basis of inappropriate aptitude tests, to a 'blue collar' education in lower tracks distinctly unequal to that provided white children in upper tracks.

[15] *Ibid.*, p. 289–90.
[16] Nathaniel Hicherson, "Physical Integration is not Enough," *Journal of Negro Education* (Spring 1966), p. 114.

Many Negro schools had no honors track and few white schools had the 'basic' or lowest track." [17]

The tracking system does not appear to benefit the bright child. Dr. Pearl states, "Both here and in England, it appears that a bright child learns no better when placed with a bunch of bright kids than when grouped heterogeneously." [18] Other studies confirm these results. And tracking certainly places those students in the lower tracks at a disadvantage. Low track assignment is destructive to a child's self-concept. In Scotland an IBM computer was incorrectly programmed, sending the "slow" students into the high track and the "bright" ones into the low track. About one year later, when the mistake was discovered, authorities found that the "slow pupils were behaving as though they were bright and the 'bright' pupils were behaving as though they were stupid." [19]

Most remedial tracks provide an inferior education which only serves to increase the gap between high- and low-track students. The idea has been that if a child is behind, he is "slow" and must be taught slowly. Instead of providing compensatory, catch-up work, this drags the student still further behind while the duller curriculum destroys any interest he might have had in his studies. Educator Edward Passow says of this process, "Making the content simpler—watering it down—has not contributed to upgrading achievement nor has it resulted in any greater involvement in school learning." [20] A résumé of one of the recently published junior high texts in American history states:

> As in a number of the other texts directed at slower readers or students, the topic of the Negro, as with all other topics for the most part, is inadequate in space and superficial in content. The irony is that these students are cheated as much if not more than if they were more able than they are. At least the faster students may fill in gaps through their own initiative. Under the circumstances, the

[17] Paul Lauter and Florence Howe, "The School Mess," *New York Review of Books*, Feb. 1, 1968, p. 17, review of A. Harry Passow and others, *Toward Creating a Model School System*.

[18] Pearl, p. 5.

[19] *Ibid.*, p. 5.

[20] Passow, p. 361.

texts aimed at this level do a more damaging job than the so-called
" 'superior student' oriented book." [21]

The first "integrated" readers brought out by the Detroit schools,
the "Play with Jimmy, Fun with David, and Laugh with Larry"
series for inner-city schools, contained about half the vocabulary
of those used in suburban schools, because the inner-city child's
"normal" English was found to be about half the size of the middle-
class first grader's. The white education "experts" were once again
caught in the trap of believing ghetto children to be in need of
"remedial" education, when the true need was for material that
was relevant to ghetto life. Black children do not need books with
less vocabulary, but with *different* vocabulary and different stories
that use the language they speak. Once children have learned to
read and to be familiar with words, it is easy for them to pick up
the vocabulary of the white community if they need to do so.

Ability grouping insures that the black ghetto child will be locked
into the definition of "slowness" imposed by a biased IQ test. Tracking condemns the average black child to an inferior, low-track
education. In addition, tests and tracking contribute indirectly to
the reduction of the quality of his education through their adverse
influence on important motivational factors such as the black child's
self-concept and the attitudes and expectations of his teacher.

TEACHER ATTITUDES

Children readily perceive their teachers' attitudes and expectations toward them. One author reports: "They (the children) were
telling me about the expressions on teachers' faces that they didn't
like. They reported that they knew the minute they entered the
room that the teacher didn't like them and that she didn't think
they were going to do too well in school." [22]

Studies show that children may be greatly affected by what their

[21] Irving Sloan, *The Negro in Modern American History Textbooks*,
(Washington, D.C.: American Federation of Teachers, AFL–CIO, 1967),
p. 17.
   [22] Riessman, p. 6.

teachers think the children can accomplish. Kenneth Clark states, "Stimulation and teaching based on positive expectation seem to play an even more important role in a child's performance in school than does the community environment from which he comes." [23] In a recent study in a South San Francisco school with a large majority of low socioeconomic status Mexican-American students, teachers in the lower grades were told that certain children (randomly picked by the experimenters) were "potential academic spurters." Tests were administered to the supposed "spurters" and to a control group at the beginning of the school year and several times during the next two years. "The results indicated strongly that children from whom teachers expected greater intellectual gains showed such gains." [24] The gains were greatest in the first and second grades, where children's self-concepts were still malleable. The average gain of the randomly picked "spurters" was over 27 IQ points. At the end of the first year, the "spurters" were described by their teachers "as having a better chance of being successful in later life and as being happier, more curious and more interesting than other children. There was also a tendency for the designated children to be seen as more appealing, better adjusted and more affectionate, and as less in need of social approval. In short, the children for whom intellectual growth was expected became more alive and autonomous intellectually, or were at least so perceived by their teachers." [25]

By contrast, teacher ratings given to those children who had not been marked as "spurters" but who did gain in IQ were generally unfavorable. The more these children gained, the less favorably were they rated by their teachers. The study concluded that children who gain intellectually when improvement is not expected of them "are looked on as showing undesirable behavior." [26] A disturbing implication of this finding has to do with the rigidity of stereotypes derived from presumed ability group labels.

This study challenges the notion that the school system allows

[23] Kenneth Clark, *Dark Ghetto* (New York: Harper & Row, 1965), p. 132.
[24] Robert Rosenthal and Lenore F. Jacobson, "Teacher Expectations for the Disadvantaged," *Scientific American*, 218 (April 1968), p. 22.
[25] *Ibid.*, p. 22.
[26] *Ibid.*, p. 22.

the child to "develop at his own pace." On the contrary, it appears that once the child's intellectual ability is "fixed" by his IQ test score and his teachers form an opinion of his potential, his intellectual growth is largely determined. For the black student, such a combination of testing procedures, ability grouping, and teachers' stereotypes can prove disastrous. The practices of the institution trap him into an inferior education. Dr. Pearl eloquently summarizes: "The teacher's responsibility is to teach, but instead we engage in self-fulfilling prophecy. We decide that certain people cannot be educated. We refuse to educate them; they grow up uneducated and we pride ourselves on our exceedingly predictive index." [27]

Dr. Pearl's observation hits hardest at teachers. There is, of course, little doubt that teacher expectations strongly influence student self-images and therefore the student's ability to learn in the classroom. And it is commonly assumed that teachers have preferences where their pupils are concerned. To expect other than this from teachers is to deny them the right to be human. It is unfortunate, however, that teacher expectations and preferences are often influenced by racial and class stereotypes. Teachers are frequently infected by what Murray Wax has called the "vacuum ideology," the belief that children are different because they have been deprived of what is desirable. The "vacuum ideology" has greatest implications for those who differ from teachers in both economic status and race—the black poor. It is not uncommon for white lower-middle or middle-class teachers, who aspire to middle- or upper-middle-class status, to choose as their favorites students who belong to the present or aspired-to class. Negro children, then, are dismissed as being intellectually and psychologically different. This perceived difference is too often spelled "inferior."

One interesting study has shown that white teachers have attitudes which prevent them from effectively dealing with black students. In this survey more than half of the white teachers in a ghetto school described their students as "lazy" while only 19 per cent of the black teachers did so; 39 per cent of the white teachers viewed the students as "high-strung" while only 3 per cent

²⁷ Pearl, p. 3.

of the black teachers so described them. "Generally, white teachers tend to avoid those adjectives which reflect stability and the types of qualities one would desire of children in the formal classroom setting. Negro teachers, on the other hand, select items which seem to be universal attributes of children (i.e., energetic, fun-loving, and happy) in addition to those which appear to go hand in hand with a successful learning experience (i.e., ambitious and coopera-tive)." [28]

The white teachers in the study were found to be generally more dissatisfied with their jobs than the black teachers. Further-more, the reasons for dissatisfaction for black teachers "tend to emphasize problems related to the physical setting of the school, while white teachers are more likely to stress problems pertaining to the shortcomings of the students." [29] In Washington, D.C., public schools, approximately two-fifths of the teachers cited low student intelligence as a factor which interferes with teaching and learn-ing.[30] Of course a child is not likely to respond favorably to a teacher he feels does not like him and who believes he cannot learn. Writing of prejudiced white teachers, Joseph Kirkman says: "Such teachers generally have a continual discipline problem with their classes. It appears that the children sense their teachers' attitude toward them and react accordingly. . . . I have yet to see any teacher who does not respect his students, have respect shown to him." [31]

Many teachers expect bad behavior of ghetto children, and there-fore they receive it. Most ghetto children have had bad experiences with teachers. Many children's reactions to teachers and school on the whole have become negative. Biased teacher attitudes have created a syndrome of failure and rebellion in the ghetto child's experiences with school. The new teacher thus finds ghetto children just as unruly as he was told they would be. He clamps down on discipline out of a fear of losing control, thus confirming the child-

[28] D. Gottlieb, "Teaching and Students: The Views of Negro and White Teachers," *Sociology of Education,* 37 (1964), 353.

[29] *Ibid.,* p. 350.

[30] Lauter and Howe, p. 18.

[31] J. Kirkman, "White Teacher in a Negro School," *Journal of Negro Education* (Spring 1966), p. 179.

ren's expectations of school and teachers. The result is perpetuation of a custodial school system, one which keeps children in line and off the streets but makes little effort to teach them.

THE NEED FOR COMMUNITY CONTROL

The lack of black control of black schools is one of the chief causes for the specific malpractices and their ugly consequences. The failure of many black children to achieve competence in the basic skills such as reading and writing cannot be overcome simply through peripheral black culture programs. It is reasonable to presume that significant improvement will occur only when black people can look upon the schools as institutional expressions of their own aspirations, not as remote white structures that intrude into their lives.

The recent Coleman Report found that the degree of faith students have in their school's ability to help them shape their own futures has a "stronger relationship to achievement than . . . all the [other] school factors together." [32] The Riot Commission states that "school administrators, teachers, parents and the students themselves . . . regard ghetto schools as inferior. Reflecting this attitude, students attending such schools lose confidence in their ability to shape their future." [33] Ironically for black students this "destiny-control" factor rises in proportion to the number of whites in the school. [34] White middle-class parents have the power to insist on and receive good schooling for their children and it is not improbable that black students realize this. Black people do not have such leverage.

The demand for community control of schools must be acknowledged and accepted if an educational reform program is to have any meaning. The Riot Commission appears to recognize this when it says that school districts should maintain "centralized control over educational standards and the raising of revenue, while de-

[32] *Equality of Educational Opportunity,* p. 23.
[33] *Ibid.,* p. 427.
[34] *Ibid.,* p. 23.

centralizing control over other aspects of educational policy." But when the Report proceeds to discuss specific changes, it becomes clear that the Commission does not follow through with the changes that will be necessary to achieve this goal. The Commission suggests programs that do not include substantive changes, and it is not made clear whether these programs are to originate within the ghetto or to be imposed upon it. For example, the Report suggests the use of local residents as tutors and teacher aides because "these workers can contribute to improving community-school relations by providing a close link between the school system and the parents." For preschool education, the Report also recommends the use of community education classes, community aides, and mothers' assistants. *The effect of these programs still depends upon who controls curriculum and other policy decisions.* Various forms of low-level community participation when unaccompanied by real shifts in power on the decision-making level have the effect of making the community respond to the schools instead of making the schools respond to the desires of the community. They attempt to treat the symptoms of hostility without doing away with its causes. The basic system of white-controlled ghetto schools remains. Such programs *may* temporarily ease tension, but they do not bring the necessary self-determination to black people.

Chapter 4

The Miseducation of White Children

Education in a democratic society must equip the children of the nation to realize their potential and to participate fully in American life. For the community at large, the schools have discharged this responsibility well.

REPORT OF THE NATIONAL ADVISORY
COMMISSION ON CIVIL DISORDERS

The preceding chapter indicated how our public schools have provided a vastly substandard education for black children. The inadequacy of ghetto schools has been well documented in the Kerner Report and other studies. But, as the above quotation illustrates, there is no recognition of the miseducation of white children.

The most affluent, best-equipped schools present white children with a distorted view of black people and other races. Textbooks do not even touch on the depth and pervasiveness of racism within the white community. It is almost as though we were indoctrinating our children rather than helping them to learn for themselves what the world of people is all about. As John Holt says in *How Children Fail*, ". . . we are not honest about ourselves, our own fears, limitations, weaknesses, prejudices, motives. We present ourselves to children as if we were gods, all-knowing, all-powerful, always rational, always just, always right." [1] Such an education, rather than preparing white children to recognize, understand, and deal with the racial contradiction in our society, glosses over it as though

[1] John Holt, *How Children Fail* (New York: Dell, 1964), p. 170.

it did not exist or was not of major importance. Children are brought up to accept America's racism and yet to "believe in" freedom, justice, and equality for all. Social studies textbooks, because they provide a common element in teaching in many classrooms of many schools, are prime contributors to the institutional racism which pervades white education.

AMERICAN HISTORY

In their treatment of racial matters, American history textbooks present an idealized and distorted picture of the national state of affairs. In the past the general public (most teachers and school administrators included) has either been unaware of the "great lie of silence," as Mark Twain put it, or has chosen to let half-truths remain as educational content. Although there recently have been efforts to correct errors and to include the black American in textbooks, these efforts still fall far short of a fair treatment. The new texts, although less overtly racist than the old, are marked by the same inability to acknowledge the historical and present disparity between our stated ideals and actual institutional practices. This lack of a self-critical perspective extends to the treatment of other societies, particularly the nonwhite, non-Western, nonindustrialized cultures, which are evaluated in terms of their acceptance or rejection of white American values.

The treatment of American minority groups in traditional textbooks has been abominable, with publishers catering to the "Southern view." A study by the Anti-Defamation League covering the twenty-four major secondary school U.S. history texts in 1949 and again in 1961 showed that the treatment of Asiatic and Spanish-speaking minorities had improved steadily if slowly, although there was still much distortion in the 1961 texts. However, the position of the Negro in texts over this period had not changed; he remained "invisible." [2]

A study of the texts used in California public schools in 1964

[2] Lloyd Marcus, "The Treatment of Minorities in Secondary School Textbooks" (New York: Anti-Defamation League, 1961), pp. 38–48.

showed the same results: "While the authors of the books must know that there are Negroes in America and have been since 1619, they evidently do not care to mention them too frequently. In one book there is no account of slavery in the colonial period; in a second, there is not a single word about Negroes after the Civil War; in a third (composed of documents and substantive chapters), the narrative does not mention Negroes in any connection."[3]

In treating the history of race relations, the authors of these texts take pains not to mention anything that might cause disagreement among whites. The 1964 survey continues: ". . . all the texts play down or ignore the long history of violence between Negroes and whites, suggesting that racial contacts have been characterized by a 'progressive harmony.' In their blandness and amoral optimism, these books implicitly deny the obvious deprivations suffered by Negroes. In several places they go further, implying approval for the repression of Negroes or patronizing them as being unqualified for life in a free society."[4]

The textbooks consistently ignore or stereotype the black man's present position in America as well as his historical role. In the Anti-Defamation League's study, three-fourths of the books mention blacks somewhere, but only half refer to them in present society. One-fourth (six books) give the name of some contemporary black. Of these, one mentions only a baseball player, and one limits its coverage to two prizefighters.

The scanty coverage of recent events usually lacks sufficient background material to be understandable. For instance, half of the books mention the Supreme Court's desegregation decision in 1954. But only two books give any consideration to the underlying principles and to the ongoing attempts at evasion.

Since 1963 the pressure of the civil rights movement has brought a rash of new "integrated" textbooks. These "multi-ethnic" texts are less overtly racist and include more Negro history and some treatment of the civil rights movement and of black people's position in contemporary America. Yet the texts fall short of an accurate state-

---

[3] Kenneth M. Stampp, Winthrop D. Jordan, *et al.*, "The Negro in American History Textbooks," unpublished paper accepted unanimously by the California State Board of Education on March 12, 1964, p. 2.
[4] *Ibid.*, pp. 2–3.

ment of white individual and institutional racism and of the life and struggles of black people throughout the history of America.

For the most part, the new multi-ethnic texts are limited to a self-conscious correction of past mistakes rather than presenting a coherent reinterpretation of American history. A study produced by the American Federation of Teachers (AFL–CIO) of junior and senior high texts published up to December, 1967, points out the uneven treatment in the new texts.[5] Not only do they vacillate between accuracy and overt racist distortion, but they also frequently contain 200- and 300-page gaps with no mention of black people. Often those minority people and events covered are dealt with very briefly and with no depth of understanding.

A shortcoming even more serious than the inconsistent and superficial treatment of black people in American history is the misleading optimism which pervades coverage of racial matters. The authors of the new books assume that assimilation of blacks into the present American society is possible and desired by both blacks and whites. In accord with this assumption the authors minimize individual racism, ignore institutional racism, and exaggerate white support for the black struggle. In addition, they fail to mention any black political or cultural forces that assert an ethnic or cultural identity of their own or that are directed toward any other goal than assimilation into white America.

The new texts emphasize what whites have done in the civil rights movement, but they play down the extent and violent nature of white opposition to the struggle for equality. Thus, the books stress legislation, the area in which whites have done most of their work for civil rights. But the legislative loopholes and the nonenforcement of civil rights laws are largely ignored. Furthermore, the texts do not recognize the problems which legislation alone cannot solve, problems such as unemployment, police brutality, or lack of access to positions of power.

The cumulative impact of these errors in the texts is a superficially optimistic outlook. For example, a senior high text capsulizes the recent decades:

[5] Irving Sloan, *The Negro in Modern American History Textbooks*, 2nd ed. (Washington, D.C.: American Federation of Teachers, AFL–CIO, 1967).

Following both World War I and World War II, millions of Negroes moved to Northern cities. As voters and officeholders there, they were able to wield great political influence. Many Negroes joined organizations whose main purpose was to obtain for Negroes "equal protection of the laws" in all respects. As more and more Negroes got a better education and improved their economic status in both North and South, they demanded an end to all discrimination. Many whites, many of them influential, supported their cause.[6]

And that is the end of the text's coverage. Such a passage exaggerates grossly the meager powers blacks have gained within the American system, leaving the impression that a black-white coalition is rapidly and smoothly eliminating domination and discrimination. It ignores the fact that with the concentration of the black population in deteriorating city ghettos, racial inequities have become more obvious and racial tensions have grown correspondingly.

Even the history text *Land of the Free*, which was commended by the AFT pamphlet for its treatment of the civil rights movement, exaggerates the role of whites, particularly the federal government.[7] The text implies that the "important advances" which have theoretically been made came about through action by the federal government which would have occurred without the demonstrations:

Nowhere does it [the Constitution] call for demonstrations. Yet without the demonstrations, Presidents Kennedy and Johnson *might* not have called *so effectively* for the Civil Rights Act of 1964 or President Johnson *so eloquently* for the Voting Act of 1965.[8]

In fact, fifty years of pressure by the NAACP, SCLC, SNCC, CORE, and other organizations through legal suits, speeches, and demonstrations were necessary before the President or Congress found it relevant or politically necessary to put their stamp of approval on any such legislation.

When giving coverage to a demonstration such as the 1963 March

[6] *Ibid.*, p. 28.
[7] John W. Caughey, John Hope Franklin, and Ernest R. May, *Land of the Free* (Pasadena, California: Franklin Publications, Inc., 1967).
[8] *Ibid.*, p. 615, italics added.

on Washington, *Land of the Free* gives credit only to Martin Luther King, although CORE and SNCC were the major organizers. Again and again texts play down those organizations whose views or methods are outside the bounds of that which the dominant white community judges to be an acceptable means of dissent. *Land of the Free* also assumes that the federal government is actively enforcing the legislation. Yet nonenforcement of integration laws has been the government's *de facto* policy since the end of Reconstruction.[9]

No mention is made in any of the texts of the deeply imbedded Jim Crow system which originated and developed in the North while Southern blacks were still slaves. Most important, none of the new texts recognize the racism imbedded in the institutions of American society today. The texts treat black people as though they were one of the immigrant groups. Immigrants, the authors of *Land of the Free* state, became part of the national community because they "all were committed to being Americans," and thus were willing to give up their old ways.[10] The unstated corollary is that as blacks become "Americanized" they will enter the mainstream of society. This argument by analogy overlooks the barriers which racism has placed between black people and participation in American society. Furthermore, it assumes that a process of "Americanization" must take place that includes the abandonment of cultural and ethnic identity. On the one hand, it is important to keep in mind that white immigrant groups have by no means been forced to give up their ethnic ties before assuming positions of power and influence. On the other, it must be at least considered as a possibility that black cultural and racial identity are stronger and more essential to the black community than are the bonds of any white group in America. The failure to understand white racism and the reality of ethnic identity leaves high school students with the mistaken notion that the racial crisis is a "Negro problem" rather than a white problem.

Not only do the new texts present assimilation into white society as presently feasible for blacks, but they also imply that assimilation has been the goal of all black politics and culture. The books men-

[9] See Chap. 8, pp. 116–118.
[10] Caughey, *et al.*, p. 425.

tion only those trends in black thought and action which can be readily accepted by whites, those which fit into the "mainstream" of American life. Even *Land of the Free*, a book attacked in some quarters for its "excessive" coverage of Negro history, illustrates this whitewashing of black politics and culture.[11]

In dealing with the civil rights movement, *Land of the Free* emphasizes the Supreme Court decision on school integration in 1954 and the work of Martin Luther King (the only black named as a leader of demonstrations). There is considerable space devoted to the programs of Booker T. Washington, but only passing reference to W. E. B. DuBois, a founder of the NAACP, who came much closer to demanding full human rights for black people. DuBois' demands were unacceptable to the whites in power. His forthright attack on American racism is as repugnant to the whites in control of textbooks today as it was during his lifetime. Militant organizations such as CORE and SNCC and the black separatist movements of Marcus Garvey, the Black Muslims, and Malcolm X are entirely ignored. Thus the text brings the struggle for black liberation into the American system by stressing white participation and government support, while failing to recognize any leaders or groups which asserted black identity or demanded more than white America was ready to allow. This approach does not convey the severity of the oppression or the bitterness of the struggle for self-determination; it also leaves the white student without an awareness of the rapidly growing trend toward black consciousness and self-rule in the black community.

Coverage of the culture of black people is negligible. Only those areas are covered which have influenced the tastes and values of white America. For example, in *Land of the Free* blues are not mentioned at all, and jazz is mentioned only insofar as it was popular in mainstream America in general in the 1920's. The text mentions no black musicians or athletes, presumably because the California Curriculum Commission has ordered that books should help pupils to refrain from attempts at stereotyping. Admittedly, a discussion of black musicians and athletes alone would not be adequate coverage of black culture, but their exclusion has not been

---

[11] Several well known periodicals carry the story of the opposition to the *Land of the Free* when it became a California state textbook.

balanced by the inclusion of black authors, artists, and social thinkers. Stereotyping is not remedied by reducing the amount of information but by increasing its volume and scope.

FOREIGN HISTORY

The "ethnocentrism" of white American society affects the way our textbooks treat not only whites and blacks in America, but also how they treat the history and culture of other peoples. The attitudes that one's own race, nation, and culture are superior to all others may be natural but nevertheless very dangerous beliefs. American textbooks generally treat European cultures as basically the same as our own with the addition of the accumulated ornaments of antiquity. However, when dealing with areas beyond the white, Western world, the authors change their approach significantly.

The treatment of people of color in nonindustrialized countries, even in the new textbooks, denies the existence of fully integrated cultures based upon values and institutions different from our own. An anthropologist from a major university who had just received the edited version of a fourth-grade monograph on a south sea island culture remarked that "as usual, the editors have cut everything that was actually different from American culture." He commented further that he always had to tone down cultural differences when writing and that publishers, hoping to sell their books widely, cut out most of what was left.

Let us take the elementary school children in California schools as an example. They are exposed to African culture in the regular curriculum only through two short chapters in the seventh-grade *Eurasia*[12] and, if their school has purchased them, through two supplementary books—one a seventh-grade supplement to *Eurasia* entitled *Africa*.[13] The brevity of coverage would be partially ex-

[12] Robert M. Glendinning, and Marguerite U. Hley, *Eurasia: Lands and Peoples of the World* (Boston: Ginn and Company, 1958).

[13] William D. Allen, *Africa* (Sacramento, California: California State Department of Education, 1964).

cusable if the material were fair. But a survey of *Eurasia* and *Africa*
shows how our racism, ethnocentrism, and paternalism are inter-
woven.

Eurasia begins: "Until about sixty years ago, Africa was often
spoken of as the Dark Continent." The rest of the chapter makes
it clear that, thanks to white efforts, this name is becoming less
appropriate. The history of Africa in both this and the supplementary text is the story of how Europeans "discovered" and
developed Africa.

In *Africa* there is not a single discussion of a traditional African
culture that gives a sense of different values and another way of
life from that in America. The very categories into which the
discussion of African life is divided do not allow for other than
an ethnocentric presentation. Following a single chapter on the
races and ecology of African people, the headings for the rest of
the book are "Farming and Grazing," "Natural Resources," "Industry," "Transportation," "Cities of Africa," and "Education and
Health." Thus the book deals almost entirely with technology and
economy, the most important factors in American eyes and the
dimensions of society in which Africa suffers most by comparison.

Despite the fact that anthropologists and historians now document the existence of highly organized civilizations with complex
legal systems in sub-Sahara Africa for the last fifteen to twenty cen-
turies,[14] *Africa* suggests continually that Africans did not know
how to govern themselves until Europeans instructed them: "As
more Africans became educated and learned about life in the rest of
the world, they came to believe that they would have better lives
if they could govern themselves. . . . In some parts of Africa, the
people do not yet know how to govern themselves in a peaceful,
orderly way. . . . The British government has worked hard to train
the people in its colonies for self-government." [15] These passages
continue the stereotype of the Dark Continent to which benevolent
Europeans brought the gift of enlightenment.

There is no recognition of the rights of African people. These
books discuss colonization without one word as to what Africans
felt about this usurpation and exploitation of themselves, their

[14] Basil Davidson, *The Lost Cities of Africa* (Boston: Little, Brown,
1959).
[15] Allen, pp. 53–54.

resources, and their cultures. The struggle against European domination and the process of gaining independence are mentioned
only with the doubtful comment that where tribes have had little
contact with the outside world, "they are greatly puzzled by the
changes and often resentful of coming foreigners." [16] It is not asked
why foreigners are invading the territory.

Western influence is lumped together under the heading of
"modernization" and is implicitly considered good: "Since 1900
great changes have taken place in Africa, and changes are continuing rapidly today. People from other continents are penetrating to
all parts of Africa. They are bringing with them modern ideas and
modern ways of living and working." [17] The books do not admit
the exploitation of African labor and resources and the destruction
of native culture that have accompanied foreign modernization.
In *Africa's* single attempt to pay homage to traditional craftsmen,
the handmade goods are admitted to be "beautiful," but "craftsmen cannot produce the things needed for a modern way of life." [18]
The implication is that the acquisition of a European way of life
is the only acceptable social goal, and therefore the craftsmen must
be replaced.

Given the assumption that modernization has first priority and
the fact that Africa's people "do not have the money or equipment
to build dams, power plants, industries, schools, hospitals, and other
things that they must have to become modern nations," [19] it follows
that Africans must be dependent on the paternalism of white
Western nations. In this view, just as the Africans needed Europeans to show them how to govern themselves, they now "need"
Europeans to show them how to build up their countries. Thus the
texts prepare the way for a very favorable presentation of current
white paternalism toward Africa. "People in other parts of the
world are trying to help the nations of Africa. Britain, France, and
other former colonial powers are lending money and sending en-
gineers and other skilled workers to Africa. The United Nations,
the United States, and the Soviet Union are also giving aid." [20]
Pictures show European foremen instructing African laborers. The

[16] Glendinning and Hley, p. 324.
[17] *Ibid.*, p. 315.
[18] Allen, p. 116.
[19] *Ibid.*, pp. 54–55.
[20] *Ibid.*, p. 55.

greater part of *Africa* is spent in discussing the dams, schools, industries, and roads which white men have either built or shown Africans how to build.

Underlying the treatment of nonwhite cultures in *Eurasia* and *Africa* are the assumptions that white values and forms of government are by nature good and must be shared with the less fortunate nonwhites of the world. Africans are presented not as having a *different* culture and way of life from white Americans, but as having *no* culture worth saving. Africans may be seen as "good" only when they have adopted the "modern" white way of life. Until then people of color should be grateful to whites for their generosity in helping them to become "white." The presentation in the new texts is merely a continuation of the old "white man's burden" notion in more subtle form. But the use of "modern," "Western," and "European" in place of "white" does not change the fact of underlying racism. Through books such as these, American school children today are acquiring the same sense of white superiority to other cultures that their parents and grandparents learned from lessons about "savages" and the "Dark Continent." In a manner similar to the new American history textbooks, *Eurasia* and *Africa* carry on the racism of their predecessors in a form that is less overt but just as false and dangerous.

CONCLUSION

The distortions taught in our schools have not been caught and changed largely because whites control curriculum even in most overwhelmingly minority areas. Most books are selected at the state or the school district level, neither of which have anywhere near proportional representation of minority groups. Moreover, regardless of who controls selection, the choice is limited to books written, edited, and published by whites concerned with profit. The standards have been fairly clear, though unstated, and most of the coercion polite. The author, interested in selling his books, has usually done the cutting himself. As Jules Henry pointed out, "the same fear, the same self-serving, governs those who make the book as it governs those who have the power to say 'yes' or 'no' to the publication of a book."

In summary, our public schools, through the use of racist text-books written, edited, published, selected, and taught by whites, are inculcating into white children false notions of superiority over people of color by presenting a distorted view of the historical and contemporary roles of whites and nonwhites in the world. In addition, our schools teach children an attitude of optimism toward race relations, a notion that "things aren't really so bad" and "everything will work out" if we just keep on as we have been doing. Our school system, like our society in general, fails to recognize that the ideals of justice and equality for all cannot be achieved without fundamental change in the institutions of white America.

This chapter has concentrated on a few textbooks in order to show in some detail what children are exposed to in school. We have deliberately refrained from picking the worst points from a wide selection of texts. Although concentrating here on textbooks, on the assumption that textbooks are the most concrete source of classroom information, it should be remembered that textbooks do not teach children. The well-informed teacher can instil understanding in her students irrespective of biases and prejudices in textbooks, and the poorly informed teacher, especially if she herself has racial prejudices, can undermine even the best text.

Most teachers are between these two extremes. Often they recognize the problem, but have neither the time nor resources to revise their understanding of U.S. history, either in the domestic sphere or in U.S. foreign policies. The vast majority of today's adult generation grew up with textbooks and classroom instruction far more prejudiced in content than that represented by *Eurasia* and *Africa*. Often the parents who want to see that their children mature free of racial prejudices and distortions do not have a full understanding of how the myth of racial superiority is bound up in the history of nearly all white nations of the world. These parents are not prepared to accept the major changes that must come about in education to create a truly non-racist program.

Even a new analysis of history and world affairs will not automatically bring either the teacher or the parent to the point where he no longer communicates covertly racist attitudes to the child. Such covert communication will continue until teachers of the young become conscious of a racist bias at the personal and psychological level as well as at the factual and analytic level.

Chapter 5

Racism in the Administration of Justice

It is often said that law is the foundation of our society. Law sets forth commonly accepted standards of behavior in written form so that social controls may be applied in an orderly and consistent way. For most Americans the legal system works fairly well. The written standards of conduct and the police and judicial apparatus set up to enforce them are established and administered by persons with interests and perspectives similar to those of the majority of white Americans. But for those who differ substantially in economic status or culture from the white middle-class norm, the apparatus breaks down. Not only are these people arrested and prosecuted under laws they had no hand in making, but they are also tried by judicial institutions which exclude them both from structural mechanisms and from personnel rolls.

The situation is most acute for those who are both poor and culturally different—blacks, Indians, and Mexican-Americans. To these citizens the law symbolizes white oppression. Those who represent the legal system are almost exclusively white and reflect the prejudices and ignorance of white society. Yet the problem is much deeper than one of participation in judicial functions. The very structures of the system, because they were created by whites, invariably operate to disadvantage the culturally different, regardless of who is in control. The unequal dispensation of justice is a result both of the origin of legal institutions and their present operation by white citizens who do not recognize the worth of nonwhite cultures. The effects of these two factors are impossible to disentangle. We emphasize the racism of the legal structures themselves because it is more basic than the personal racism of administrators and thus has more profound implications as an obstacle to change.

THE POLICE AND THE BLACK COMMUNITY

It is no accident that many of the major ghetto riots of the past few years have been triggered by incidents with the police. White-controlled structures of business and government are, for the most part, invisible within the ghetto itself. The landlord appears only once or twice a month to collect rent, and the local merchants leave for their homes in the suburbs after business hours. But the police officer is present around the clock. In fact, because of the high crime rate, the ghetto is the scene of the most intense police activity in the city. Hence, even without considering the quality of police patrol practices, it is clear that the police officer is still the white man seen most often by the ghetto residents.

The President's Commission, after its study of the riots of the summer of 1967, pointed out that the residents of the ghettos perceived police brutality and harassment as their greatest grievance, greater in intensity than either unemployment or housing. It is clear that most of these charges against the police are justified, as well as those made by the President's Commission on Law Enforcement and Administration of Justice, which pointed out the extreme prejudice shown by almost half of the police officers working in Negro areas of northern cities.

Much of the friction between law officers and the black community stems from the overwhelming whiteness of most police departments. The following statistics taken from the Report of the National Advisory Commission on Civil Disorders clearly indicate the situation:

PER CENT NONWHITE POLICE AND PER CENT NONWHITE
POPULATION OF SOME MAJOR CITIES [1]

Name of Department	Per Cent of City's Nonwhite Population	Per Cent of Nonwhite Police
Atlanta, Ga.	38	10
Baltimore, Md.	41	7
Boston, Mass.	11	2
Buffalo, N.Y.	18	3
Chicago, Ill.	27	17
Cincinnati, Ohio	28	6
Cleveland, Ohio	34	7
Dayton, Ohio	26	4
Detroit, Mich.	39	5
Hartford, Conn.	20	11
Kansas City, Mo.	20	6
Louisville, Ky.	21	6
Memphis, Tenn.	38	5
Michigan State Police	9	*
New Haven, Conn.	19	7
New Orleans, La.	41	4
New York, N.Y.	16	5
New Jersey State Police	9	*
Newark, N.J.	40	10
Oakland, Calif.	31	4
Oklahoma City, Okla.	15	4
Philadelphia, Pa.	29	20
Phoenix, Ariz.	8	1
Pittsburgh, Pa.	19	7
St. Louis, Mo.	37	11
San Francisco, Calif.	14	6
Tampa, Fla.	17	3
Washington, D.C.	63	21

* Less than one-half of 1 per cent.

When we look at the supervisory personnel of the various police departments, this picture becomes even more serious. The percentage of nonwhite sergeants, lieutenants, and captains is significantly lower than the above figures which represent the racial make-up of the whole department. For example, only in April, 1968, did San Francisco, with a total force of 1,754 men, name its

[1] *Report of the National Advisory Commission on Civil Disorders,* p. 321.

first Negro sergeant.[2] Needless to say, there are no Negro lieutenants or captains on the San Francisco force. Thus, because almost all law enforcement personnel are white, ghetto residents view the law itself as white.

In recent years law enforcement agencies, particularly in the larger cities, have significantly raised their acceptance standards for new officers. These higher standards are due to the recognition of the fact that police officers under the present system must be both sophisticated crime detectors and sensitive social workers. While specific requirements vary, most departments require a high school diploma. The applicant then takes a barrage of written, oral, and physical examinations. If he successfully completes these, he next takes a course of several months duration in a police academy during which he is expected to become familiar with the myriad laws he must enforce and the various procedures from patrol to arrest to incarceration.

The trend toward better qualified police applicants has doubtlessly given the white community better law enforcement. This is reflected by the widespread attitude of trust of enforcement officials that is found in white areas, in contrast to that found in the ghettos. However, the stringent standards have made it even more difficult for a significant number of black men to find work as police officers. The inferior educations of those who attended ghetto schools makes it more difficult for blacks than whites to pass written tests. Physical fitness is often lacking because of improper nutrition or deficient medical care; and those white police administrators and other white professionals who interview the applicants are usually looking for the personality traits that reflect their own middle-class backgrounds.

Many police administrators complain that very few Negroes apply for jobs in their departments. This state of affairs is the result of the overwhelming hostility toward and lack of confidence in the police force that is so commonly found in the ghetto. The police force has been white and controlled by the white city government for so long that the black man who joins the force and works in his

[2] It is clear from the *Report on Civil Disorders* that this ratio is a normal one. See, for instance, *ibid.*, p. 322.

own neighborhood must expect to be greeted by a high level of hostility from his neighbors because they believe that he has "sold out."

WHITE CONTROL OF THE STRUCTURES OF JUSTICE

White dominance of law enforcement is not limited to the police. Rather, the experience of black people with the whole law enforcement structure, from police station to prison, confirms their belief that the law is white. Blacks are represented in substantial numbers only in the courthouse and prison janitorial service.

A survey of employment in prosecutors' offices, courts, and prisons by the Civil Rights Commission in 1963 revealed that "law enforcement agencies throughout most of the Nation are staffed exclusively or overwhelmingly by whites." [3] The Commission found that black employment was almost nonexistent in the South and, except in the District of Columbia, reached only token levels in the North and West. Black employment in federal agencies was no better than that in state agencies in the same area. [4] Where blacks were employed, they held chiefly menial positions. [5]

---

[3] U.S. Commission on Civil Rights, Report, 1963, p. 124.

[4] The 289 county prosecutors' offices in the Southern and border states employed 7 black lawyers, 3 investigators, and 2 stenographers. In the North and West, 103 prosecutors' offices employed 35 black investigators and 88 secretaries. "Twenty-seven counties employed black lawyers. Many with substantial Negro populations employed no Negroes in any professional or administrative capacity." (Report, p. 120. There were 3,100 counties in the United States in 1964. [Mourad G. Paulsen, Equal Justice for the Poor, 1964, p. 7.]) Black employment in the federal prosecuting agency was no better. The Department of Justice employed 3 black U.S. attorneys, 35 black assistant U.S. attorneys (of 778), and 34 other black attorneys (of 1,372). In Southern and border state courts there were no black judges or clerks, and 3 per cent or fewer of the jury commissioners, bailiffs, and secretaries were black. Black employment in state courts in the North and West was reported to be "considerably better," although no figures are given. (A request for exact data drew the following reply from the Commission: "Concerning our 1963 report, the original data are no longer available, having been retired to the Government Archives, and the staff members who worked on this report are no longer with this Commission. Since our study did not cover employ-

Officials commonly account for the exclusion of black citizens from the agencies of justice by saying that blacks do not apply for positions or that if they apply they are unqualified. Both explanations are partially true, and both are rooted in institutional racism. Having been reminded all their lives, by their own experiences and those of fellow blacks, that they fail to meet white standards, black citizens do not apply for jobs presumed to "belong" to white society. Those responsible for appointments and hiring encourage self-elimination when they assume that certain positions are for whites and others (menial and subordinate) for blacks. The fact that black applicants fail to meet job qualifications is due to a long cycle of racism in education and other institutions. But recognition of the fact that justice is not the only racist institution does not relieve it of its part of the responsibility to break the cycle.

Not only do black people fail to find public employment in the

---

ment in the North and West, we do not have that information.") As for federal courts, there was almost no black employment in the South and little in the North and West. Blacks held no administrative, professional, or clerical positions at state adult correctional institutions in 8 Southern and border states and only 3.5 per cent of these positions in Northern and Western States. (*Report*, pp. 120–22.) In California wardens at all of the thirteen state prisons, as well as 99 per cent of the guards, are white. (Len Holt, Esq., at a conference on Racism in the Law, San Francisco, May 4, 1968.) At federal correctional institutions black employment was less than 3 per cent in the Southern and border states and even lower in the North and West. (*Report*, p. 122.)

[5] A survey of 17 Black Belt counties with a majority of blacks in the population, but 3 per cent or fewer registered to vote, found that "the only service rendered by Negroes in the courts of justice is janitorial." (*1961 Commission on Civil Rights Report*—Voting, p. 179.) In Memphis-Shelby County, Tennessee (where the nonwhite population was 36.4 per cent in 1960), only 5 blacks are employed in the judicial system outside of the custodial service in the courthouse, where they comprise 40 of the 52 employees. (Tennessee State Advisory Committee to the U.S. Commission on Civil Rights, *Employment, Administration of Justice, and Health Services in Memphis-Shelby County, Tennessee*, August 1967, pp. 64–66.) In North Carolina, where no blacks were employed in the judicial system, but 31 of over 2,000 employees in the state prison department were black, the director stated: "Our Negro personnel have done and are doing outstanding jobs for the prison department. New Negro custodial personnel have very satisfactorily completed our training school for custodial officers and they are operating in a very competent way at the present time." (North Carolina Advisory Committee to the U.S. Commission on Civil Rights, *Equal Protection of the Laws in North Carolina*, 1959–62.)

agencies of justice, but they are also underrepresented among private attorneys and judges. Blacks comprise only 1 per cent of the lawyers in the United States, a smaller proportion than in any other occupational group. There is an average of one black lawyer for 8,000 black people as compared to a national average of one lawyer for every 625 people.[6] In the South, where until recently blacks were denied admission to the bar and are still excluded from many state and local bar associations,[7] the ratio is one to 28,000.[8] Because of financial conditions, few black lawyers are able to practice outside the large cities. Most of them serve primarily poor black clientele. Sometimes even black clients are hard to get since they "often seek out white lawyers because they feel them to be more capable, or because they feel that Negro lawyers are at a disadvantage against a white adversary and before a white judge and jury."[9] Even militant blacks like Black Panther Huey Newton recognize the advantage of being represented by a white lawyer. (Of course, there were no black law firms large enough to handle the Newton case.)[10] There are only 65 black state judges and 15 out of over 300 federal judges.

Increased representation of blacks in the legal profession does not seem likely in the near future; black enrollment in law schools is only 1.3 per cent.[11] Several top schools are now disregarding the "admittedly biased" law Standard Achievement Test and accepting all black applicants whom they consider able to complete the curriculum with special help. Some schools even have minority recruitment programs to increase the very small number of applicants. Yet they generally fail to use black recruiters. Very little has been done

[6] Hon. George W. Crockett, Jr., Judge, Recorder's Court, Detroit, at a conference on Racism in the Law, San Francisco, May 4, 1968.

[7] *Report*, pp. 118–19.

[8] Crockett.

[9] *Report*, p. 119. Mexican-Americans and Indians are also grossly underrepresented in the legal profession. There are only 200 Mexican-American attorneys in California and no native California Indian attorneys. (Jose Ramos, Esq., and George F. Duke, Esq., at a conference on Racism in the Law, San Francisco, May 4, 1968.)

[10] Richard A. Bancroft, Esq., at a conference on Racism in the Law, San Francisco, May 4, 1968. A survey of five San Francisco law firms in May showed only two black employees (secretaries) out of a total of 152 attorneys, 70–85 secretaries, and 6 clerks.

[11] Crockett.

to encourage blacks to apply by hiring more black faculty members or making the curriculum more relevant.[12] The scarcity of black lawyers and judges, whether a result of outright denial of admission to the bar or the hardships of obtaining a legal education, indicates exclusion of blacks from the practice of law.

The problem of representation on juries is complex. The number of convictions overturned by the Supreme Court in recent years indicates that systematic exclusion of blacks from juries is still practiced in some parts of the South. Undoubtedly, jury exclusion is much more prevalent than the number of cases reveals, as many lawyers never raise the issue for fear of harm to their clients or themselves.[13] Methods of racial exclusion in the South, however, are becoming more subtle,[14] while throughout the rest of the nation official requirements and economic factors reduce the number of blacks on juries. Some states require jurors to be registered voters or freeholders, own taxable property, pass literacy tests, or have no criminal record. A larger proportion of blacks than of whites is excluded by such qualifications, as well as by the financial hardship of absence from work that jury service entails.[15] In the case of grand juries, which are generally chosen from persons nominated by public officials, civic organizations, or "prominent" citizens, the likelihood of representative black participation is even smaller.[16]

[12] Preble Stolz, Esq., Boalt Hall, at a conference on Racism in the Law, San Francisco, May 4, 1968.

[13] U.S. Commission on Civil Rights, *Report—Justice*, 1961, p. 92.

[14] Among the more sophisticated methods are those of summoning blacks for jury service without placing them on the panels, and agreements between counsel, sometimes even with the open support of the judge, to remove any blacks on the panel by use of peremptory challenges. (U.S. Commission on Civil Rights, *Report—Justice*, 1961, p. 100.)

[15] U.S. Civil Rights Commission, *Report—Justice*, p. 99. Mexican-Americans are also excluded from juries in California because few can read the Constitution in English, a requirement for voter registration. (Ramos.)

[16] A typical example of grand-jury selection is the situation in Baltimore, where grand jurors are chosen by the judges of the Supreme Bench, who meet three times a year to discuss the qualifications of prospective jurors. "To obtain qualified Negro grand jurors, the judges have asked prominent colored persons to submit the names of likely members of their race." (*Report—Justice*, p. 94.) Obviously such a system will result only in token representation.

When blacks do happen to appear on jury panels in cases where the defendant is of their race, they are almost always removed by the prosecution through use of peremptory challenges.[17] The jury system, like judicial agencies and the legal profession, either through conscious prejudice or through the unintended consequences of applying apparently nonracial standards, excludes black people.

In the typical case, the black person suspected of a crime is arrested by a white police officer, brought to face a white judge, district attorney, and jury in a courtroom where the proceedings are recorded by white clerks, and upon conviction sent to a prison where the only black employees are custodians. Blacks commonly appear in the white-controlled judicial system only as violators of the law. Such a situation cannot fail to reinforce their view of the judiciary as an instrument of white oppression, nor can these conditions fail to influence the administration of justice. The result may be obvious discrimination in prosecution and sentencing. But even where white participants in the judicial process are not overtly prejudiced, the class and cultural barriers between them and the black defendant invariably put him at a disadvantage.

RACIAL BIAS

In the South it is still commonly accepted that different standards of justice apply to blacks than to whites.[18] This fact has been called

[17] Charles Garry, Esq., at a conference on Racism in the Law.

[18] The state of Southern justice is well described by Anthony Lester, a British lawyer who investigated the Southern courts in the summer of 1964:

Southern officials freely admitted to me that there are four standards of justice. First, where white is against white (apart from the absence of sufficient aid to the poor), there is equal protection of the law. Second, where Negro is against Negro, the common complaint is that Southern courts and police are too lenient. One senior official explained to me that Negroes are primitive and emotional, like children or animals, with little sense of right or wrong. If a Negro commits a crime against another Negro he will usually receive a far lighter punishment than a white against white. If anything the law therefore encourages lawlessness in Negro communities. Third,

to national attention in recent years with the increase in black protest activity and the accompanying rise in white violence. Southern
officials vigorously prosecuted and convicted civil rights protesters
for disorderly conduct and breach of the peace while ignoring the
violent acts against demonstrators committed by white segregationists.[19] Although most of the convictions were later overturned by
the Supreme Court, Southern judges operated very effectively to
discourage demonstrations by holding protesters under exorbitant
bail, requiring surety bonds (which local companies refused to
sign), imposing harsh sentence for frivolous charges, and subjecting
demonstrators to intolerable jail conditions.[20] (That such practices

---

where a white commits a crime against a Negro, he will be punished
lightly if at all, and the Negro complainant may expect reprisals.
Rape is a capital offence in all Southern States, but no white has
ever been executed for raping a Negro woman. The last time a
white was executed in Mississippi for a crime against a Negro was in
1890. Fourth, where a Negro commits a crime against a white,
especially an offence against the person, retribution is swift and
severe. The statistics on capital punishment are revealing. In Lou-
isiana, between 1900 and 1950, no Louisiana-born white man, and
only 2 out-of-State whites, were ever executed for rape, while 41
Negroes were executed for raping white women. No-one, Negro or
white, was executed for rape of a Negro woman. Since 1956, one
white has been executed (for murder), and 10 Negroes (3 for rape).
In Mississippi, since 1955, 24 Negroes have been executed, 14 for
murder, 9 for rape, and one for armed robbery. In the same period
7 whites were executed, but only one was a Mississippian. (Anthony
Lester, *Justice in the American South*, London: Amnesty International, 1965, pp. 12–13.)

[19] In most cases, blacks who attempted to integrate public facilities
were not prosecuted under clearly unconstitutional state segregation
laws but were charged with disorderly conduct or breach of the peace.
"In finding the protesters guilty, a city judge in Jackson found that,
while they had been orderly, their conduct could have provoked a breach
of the peace by others." (*Report*, 1963, p. 113.)

[20] Ronald Goldfarb, *Ransom*, New York: Harper & Row, 1965, pp.
59–88. In several instances arrested juveniles were threatened with jail
sentences unless they refused to take part in future demonstrations. (U.S.
Commission on Civil Rights, *Law Enforcement: A Report on Equal
Protection in the South*, 1965, p. 80.) A survey by the Civil Rights
Commission of lawyers in the Southern and border states indicated
that 86 per cent of respondents who had handled civil rights cases were
black. A large proportion of them defended their clients under threat
of reprisal. (*Report*, 1963, pp. 117–18.) The general attitude of Southern officials was expressed in October 1962 by the district attorney in
Baton Rouge, who told Civil Rights Commission investigators: "I'm

are not confined to the South has been recently revealed in the treatment accorded blacks arrested during the Los Angeles and Detroit rebellions.)[21]

In sharp contrast to the treatment given black civil rights protesters is the almost total failure to prosecute whites for racial violence. According to the Civil Rights Commission, there were 186 serious incidents of racial violence (including at least six murders) reported in Mississippi alone during the summer of 1964. Yet "in only a few cases were those responsible arrested or prosecuted by local authorities" and even fewer cases came to trial.[22] In cases which came to trial, "defendants were either acquitted or received suspended sentences or minimal fines." [23]

Such a double standard of justice lives on in the South because it is supported by the entire community. Sheriff, district attorney, judge, and jury need have no fear that their action (or inaction) will be condemned by a public openly dedicated to the maintenance of white supremacy.[24]

---

going to make it just as hard on these outside agitators as I can. And I don't know a judge or official who doesn't agree with me." (*Report*, 1963, p. 116.)

[21] See Robert Conot, *Rivers of Blood, Years of Darkness* (New York: Bantam Books, 1967), pp. 379–85 and *Report of the National Advisory Commission on Civil Disorders*, 1968, pp. 339–43 and 347–56.

[22] U.S. Commission on Civil Rights, *Law Enforcement*, pp. 12–13.

[23] *Ibid.*, p. 49.

[24] County and district attorneys are dependent on the sheriff as an investigator and are subject to no control by the state attorney general. The Civil Rights Commission says of this problem:

A 1932 study of Mississippi county and local government stated that "a great portion of the failure of district attorneys to perform their duties properly can be traced, not to lack of knowledge, but to a feeling of security that their actions will not be reviewed." Applied to prosecutions for racial violence, this finding still appears sound today. . . .
. . . In the few cases in which persons have been prosecuted for violence against Negroes, grand juries and petit juries—from which Negroes have been systematically excluded and which express deeply rooted community attitudes—have failed to indict or convict. (*Law Enforcement*, pp. 94, 122.)

Southern judges reflect, rather than counteract, the prejudices of their communities, at the federal as well as the state level. ". . . especially at the District Court level, segregationists are still made Federal judges. For example, J. R. Robert Elliot of Georgia, who was appointed by

Outside the South, the existence of discrimination is more difficult to prove since prosecutors, judges, and juries are less open in their racism. Many experienced attorneys, both black and white, are convinced that such discrimination does occur. They cite numerous examples of district attorneys who refuse to negotiate with lawyers representing black defendants and of judges who apply different standards to black and white defendants. Jurors, being generally less well educated than members of the legal profession, are particularly likely to be infected with prejudice in a society where half of all whites believe that Negroes have looser moral standards.[25]

CULTURAL BIAS

Aside from overt racial discrimination, there is another kind of bias which occurs because white lawyers, judges, and juries cannot deal with, and the judicial system makes no provision for, the cultural gulf between black and white Americans. Black people living in ghettos isolated from white society have developed styles

---

President Kennedy, was known at the time to have stated that he did not want 'these pinks, radicals, and black voters to outvote those who are trying to preserve our segregated laws and other traditions.' Judge W. Harold Cox of Mississippi, who was also well known for his racial views before he was recently appointed, once stated from the Bench that he was 'not interested in whether the registrar is going to give a registration test to a bunch of niggers on a vote drive.'" (Lester, p. 28.) Anthony Lester describes the typical situation in a Southern court:

In every trial which I have observed in State courts in the Deep South, Negro witnesses were called by their first names in an obviously patronizing manner, in spite of a recent decision of the U.S. Supreme Court that such a practice was unconstitutional. Whenever there was a conflict of evidence between Negro and white, the judge appeared automatically to believe the white man. On no occasion was a policeman's evidence challenged. On one occasion in Canton, Mississippi, a Negro who attempted to sit on the white side of the courtroom was rudely ordered away by a uniformed policeman. Most Negroes are not represented by counsel, yet on no occasion did I see a judge attempting to put the case for a Negro against opposing witnesses. (Lester, p. 13.)

[25] William Brink and Louis Harris, *Black and White* (New York: Simon & Schuster, 1966), p. 136.

of grooming and dress, a vocabulary, and a set of traditions that are strange and incomprehensible to most whites. A white jury called upon to evaluate the evidence surrounding an incident involving black people in their own community faces a very difficult task because of this cultural barrier. Our judicial system, which is based on the assumption of cultural homogeneity, does nothing to alleviate the problem.

Anthropologists have begun to investigate the difficulties posed by linguistic barriers in the courtroom. Daniel H. Swett of San Francisco State College recently did a study of the murder trial of a black resident of East Palo Alto. The defendant pleaded not guilty by reason of self-defense. Immediately prior to the shooting, the defendant and the deceased had engaged in the "dozens," a contest of extreme verbal aggression peculiar to urban ghetto slums in which the participants try to insult each other to the point where one is either driven to violence or to running away. The first witness stated that the deceased "put [the defendant] in the dozens." When the defense counsel tried to get the witness to clarify the term "dozens," the judge upheld the prosecution's objection that "the witness had not been qualified as an expert in semantics." Thus the jury was left to guess at the meaning of important testimony. Swett cites several other examples of words and phrases used by witnesses which had an entirely different meaning in the ghetto than in the white community.[26]

On the other side, black witnesses were often perplexed by the legal jargon of the attorneys and gave answers based on misunderstanding of the vocabulary of the courtroom. Swett describes how the credibility of the sole witness to the shooting was destroyed because he gave contradictory answers due to wrong guesses of the meaning of such terms as "misdemeanor" and "correctional institution." No one brought out the fact that his vocabulary did not include these words.

After the trial the members of the jury "indicated that the greater portion of the testimony had been totally incomprehensible to them,

[26] Daniel H. Swett, "Cross-Cultural Communications in the Courtroom: Applied Linguistics in a Murder Trial," unpublished paper presented at the Conference on Racism and the Law, San Francisco, California, December 1967, pp. 2–5.

and that the witnesses appeared to be either morons who could not understand or speak plain English, or unconscionable liars who could not be believed." [27] In this case the jury's ability to render a fair verdict was severely hampered by the lack of communication in the courtroom. There is no reason to doubt that these linguistic barriers exist in all courts serving metropolitan areas.

The influence of other factors such as hair style, dress, and bearing of black witnesses is more difficult to ascertain. But undoubtedly most white jurors react unfavorably to proud, aloof black youths with tight pants and "naturals" which they associate with black power and rebellious violence. Whites subconsciously view such assertion of cultural difference as a threat to the established order.

ECONOMIC BIAS

In addition to its operation through racial and cultural discrimination, institutional racism also acts through the built-in economic bias in the judicial system. Given the caste position of black people in American society, any institution which provides superior services to the middle and upper classes and inferior services to the lower class helps to perpetuate racism. The judicial system does its part in maintaining the subordinate status of blacks by denying equal facilities to the poor.

Of the problems facing the poor in criminal courts, as then Attorney General Robert Kennedy stated in 1964, "one of the plainest . . . is bail. Its legitimate purpose of assuring that defendants appear for trial has been distorted into a systematic injustice." [28] After reviewing studies of bail practices in Chicago, Philadelphia, New York, and Washington as well as surveys of smaller communities and federal courts, Daniel Freed and Patricia Wald conclude with regard to the setting of bail:

> Committing magistrates usually know only the charge against the defendant, and perhaps his police record. The recommendations of

[27] *Ibid.*, pp. 5–6.
[28] Quoted in Lester, p. 18.

prosecutors, though accorded great weight, are based on little if any additional information. In many localities, the police, prosecutor and judge simply adhere to a fixed schedule geared to the nature of the offense. As a rule, little or no inquiry or allowance is made for individual differences between defendants based on their likelihood to appear at trial.[29]

If bail is in fact intended to fulfill its constitutional purpose of insuring that a defendant be present at his trial,[30] the means used to determine the amount of bail certainly are inadequate. Often those least likely to appear for trial and most dangerous to society, such as professional organized criminals, make bail easily through their connections with corrupt bondsmen.[31] More important from the viewpoint of the poor defendant, the bail system as generally administered causes him and his family great personal hardship and increases his chances of being convicted and of receiving a prison sentence. In large cities approximately 40 to over 80 per cent of defendants cannot raise bail and are kept in jail from one to six or eight months before trial. During this time their income is cut off, debts accumulate, and their families may be evicted from public or private housing. (They may not be immediately eligible for welfare.)

In jail the pretrial defendant is kept under the same conditions as convicted prisoners and rarely segregated from them.[32] Usually he is dependent on the court for counsel. The preparation of his defense is hampered by restrictions on the time he may meet with his lawyer, his inability to seek witnesses, and the lack of funds for investigation. There is greater pressure on him to waive a jury trial in order to hasten disposition of his case. And the fact that he must

[29] Daniel J. Freed and Patricia M. Wald, *Bail in the United States: 1964*, p. 18. Prepared as a working paper for Nat'l. Conference on Bail & Criminal Justice, U.S. Dept. of Justice and the Vera Foundation.

[30] In many cases bail is used for other purposes. Both the New York and Philadelphia studies found that judges set high bail to give the accused "a taste of jail." In Philadelphia, "some magistrates candidly admitted that they set high bail to 'break' crime waves, keep the defendant in jail, cut him off from his narcotics supply, protect women, 'make him serve some time' even where acquittal was a certainty, or protect arresting officers from false arrest suits." (Freed and Wald, p. 11.)

[31] Goldfarb, pp. 102–9.

[32] Freed and Wald, pp. 40–44.

appear in court in prison dress accompanied by a guard may adversely affect his attitude as well as that of the jury. If he is convicted, his chances of obtaining probation are lessened since he has been separated from his family and has probably lost his job. Statistics show that defendants detained before their trials are more often convicted and less often granted probation than those free on bail.[33] The bail system clearly denies equal protection to poor defendants, a large proportion of whom are black.[34]

Another disadvantage facing the lower-class defendant is the lack of adequate counsel. The Supreme Court in *Gideon v. Wainwright* (1963) established the right to counsel of an indigent accused of a felony, but this decision still has not been applied to misdemeanor or civil cases. According to a recent American Bar Association study, only 120 of 300 counties surveyed provided counsel in misdemeanor cases.[35] Although at least half of the 300,000 persons per year charged with felonies (punishable by a year or more in prison) cannot afford lawyers, most of the 3,100 counties in the United States fail to provide adequate defense for the indigent, according to a 1964 ABA report.

Two thousand and nine hundred counties use the assigned counsel system by which the judge appoints a court-paid lawyer for the

[33] The Philadelphia study of 946 cases found that 82 per cent of the jailed defendants were convicted, but only 52 per cent of those on bail. Of those convicted, 22 per cent of the jailed sample received prison sentences compared to 59 per cent of the bailed sample. A study in New York City in 1960 found that felony convictions, broken down by type of offense, ranged from 10 to 52 per cent of the cases for bailed defendants but 14 to 78 per cent for jailed. Prison sentences were given to 48 to 78 per cent of the bailed and 88 to 100 per cent of the jailed convicts in felony cases and to 32 per cent of the bailed and 87 per cent of the jailed in misdemeanor cases. Findings were similar for federal courts. Other factors, such as prior criminal record, private or assigned counsel, and social background do not seem to account for the difference in convictions and sentences (Freed and Wald, pp. 46–48). See also Goldfarb, pp. 162–65.

[34] This situation has recently been alleviated somewhat by the passage of the 1966 Federal Bail Reform Act and the spread of bail reform projects on the model of the Vera Foundation Manhattan Bail Project in New York to a number of cities. But reform still has not reached the vast majority of poor defendants.

[35] Patricia M. Wald, *Law and Poverty: 1965* (Washington: U.S. Government Printing Office), note, p. 36.

indigent defendant from a list of volunteers.[36] Some investigators have found that uneducated defendants fail to understand their right to counsel at public expense, the advantages of having a lawyer, or even the meaning of the word "counsel." Often legal aid is not present at critical points in the judicial process. In 32 states the court does not assign counsel until arraignment. Only 5 states provide counsel at the preliminary hearing, where the case may be dismissed for lack of legally obtained evidence. In 75 of the 300 counties surveyed by the ABA, there was no provision for counsel at sentencing.[37] Here, the argument of a good lawyer is often crucial in reducing the sentence or obtaining probation.

The quality of service provided by the assigned counsel system is usually not as high as that of retained counsel. One authority states: "The assignment scheme often fails to provide experienced, dedicated, and zealous counsel. It certainly does not provide the investigations and other facilities needed for a full defense." [38] Many lawyers assigned to indigents are young, often right out of law school, with no experience in criminal cases. The low fees for this type of practice make it tempting for a court-appointed lawyer to plead his client guilty to save the time and work necessary for a long trial.[39] Funds are rarely provided for expenses of investigation or calling expert witnesses or psychiatrists. Only nine states and the District of Columbia reimburse appointed counsel for out-of-pocket expenses.[40]

The alternative public defender system used in some counties has certain advantages over the assigned counsel system. A Public

[36] Indigency is generally determined by a hurried questioning of the defendant by the judge in court. Standards are often arbitrary and uncover not whether the defendant can afford average lawyer fees, but whether he is "destitute." In San Mateo County, Calif., anyone who is employed at the time of arrest or who owns any money or property is not eligible for a court-appointed attorney.

[37] Wald, pp. 36–38.

[38] Paulsen, p. 7.

[39] Dallin H. Oaks and Warren Lehman, "Lawyers for the Poor," *Transaction*, 4, no. 8 (July/August 1967), 26.

[40] Wald, note, p. 38. Tribal Indians, even if they retain their own counsel, must have their choice approved by the Bureau of Indian Affairs, which administers the government's paternalistic Indian policies. (George F. Duke, Esq., at a conference on Racism in the Law.)

Defender has a more complete staff at his disposal than the individual practitioner, as well as files of previous cases. The Public Defender does not face the same dilemmas as a court-appointed lawyer, who, if forced to choose between spending a certain amount of time on a paying client or an indigent, will probably choose the former. But even so, the Public Defender system suffers from severe problems. The fact that the Public Defender must deal with the prosecutor and judge daily may cause him to put up less of a fight in one case to get a better deal for another client later, especially if he knows the judge to be irritated by requests for jury trials, which are lengthy and expensive.

Lack of sufficient manpower and funds often limits the effectiveness of the Public Defender. A study of the San Francisco Public Defender's office in 1962 reported that the shortage of staff and funds severely limited the time given to interviewing the client and conducting an investigation as well as usually preventing jury trials and appeals.[41]

Legal aid organizations, both private and government financed, are making admirable efforts in defending the poor. But they simply do not reach enough people. As of January 1967, thirty-two states had fewer than five legal aid offices, and fourteen states had no committee on legal aid or public defense in the state bar.[42] Legal aid groups receiving OEO funds are forbidden to take criminal cases.

Probation and parole are also weighted against the poor defendant. The adverse effect of pretrial detention on chances for obtaining probation has already been mentioned. In addition, the ABA study found that 46 of the 300 counties surveyed required payment of counsel fees as a condition of probation. Many defendants are sent to prison because they cannot pay fines. California law allows civil commitment for those unable to pay fines of $500 or more. As for parole, six states require payment of a $300 bond by out-of-state parolees. Prisoners given parole are not provided with

[41] *Report of Special Committee of the Bar Association of San Francisco Concerning the Office of the Public Defender in San Francisco*, 1962.
[42] *Directory of Legal Aid and Defender Offices and Lawyer Referral Committees and Agencies*, American Bar Association, 1967.

transportation home. Since unskilled industries generally deny jobs to ex-convicts, poorer prisoners have great difficulty obtaining employment, which is often required as a condition of parole.[43]

In domestic and juvenile cases (in which the poor are often involved) where nearly all defendants appear without counsel, the uneducated person who has difficulty expressing himself is a poor match for police officers and social workers. Particularly in juvenile cases, where vague laws give the judge wide discretion in detaining a defendant before trial and disposing of him afterward, the poor, especially the black poor, are at a disadvantage. Middle- and upper-class delinquents, if they appear in court at all, are more likely to avoid institutionalization through their parents' promises of better supervision, payment of damages, private school training, or psychiatric care. Since black children are often denied admission to private care facilities, they usually must be committed to state training schools.[44]

The administration of justice, although theoretically based on the ideal of equal protection for all, is in fact largely dependent on financial considerations. With regard to justice, as with other American commodities, the more one can pay, the better product one gets. (Except for the Philippines, no other country has a commercial bail-bond system.)[45] As long as this practice remains at the foundation of American justice, no amount of compensation in the way of releasing more indigent defendants on their own recognizance or increasing the number of legal aid offices will provide the poor with equal justice. Because a greater proportion of black than of white defendants is poor, the economic bias is racist.

All of the factors discussed, whether overt racism in prosecution and sentencing or unconscious and indirect racism acting through cultural and economic channels, contribute to the differences in judicial and prison statistics between blacks and whites.[46] At every

[43] Wald, p. 39.
[44] Wald, pp. 10–11.
[45] Goldfarb, p. 227.
[46] "We have no satisfactory national judicial statistics in the United States, but according to individual studies, mostly localized, convictions of Negroes come to three to four times their proportion in the population. From reports in *National Prison Statistics*, Negroes comprise about one-third of all prisoners, although they form only one-tenth of the

stage in the law enforcement process, from arrest to parole or execution, a greater proportion of the defendants or prisoners is black than at the previous stage. Such a situation is an inevitable consequence of a system designed to enforce laws made by whites and operating through a structure created and staffed by whites. The cultural myopia of white society permeates our judicial system, making it inherently incapable of delivering justice to people of color.

U.S. population. . . . Negroes also had more commitments to prison and served more actual time before release from state penal institutions. The average (median) number of months served before release among all states in 1951 was 25 for Negroes and 20 for whites. The disparity was greater in the Northeast (Negroes 30 months; whites 24 months) and in the West (Negroes 30; whites 19) than in the Northcentral states (Negroes 26; whites 21) or in the South (Negroes 21; whites 17).

"Combined with those facts is the knowledge that proportionally about 10 to 14 per cent more whites than Negroes are annually 'released conditionally'; that is, granted some form of parole . . . over time and in different states, between 10 and 20 per cent more Negroes than whites are executed" of those sentenced to death. (Marvin E. Wolfgang, *Crime and Race, Conceptions and Misconceptions*, New York: Institute of Human Relations Press, American Jewish Committee, 1964, pp. 32 and 49.)

Chapter 6

Racism in Our Political Institutions

Institutional racism has created conditions against which black citizens are rebelling. It is to be expected that a major part of this rebellion will take political forms, for it is a well established and honored custom in America that complaints against society are to be redressed in the political arena. Unfortunately, a serious political obstacle immediately confronts the black in his attempt to use political means to redress social, economic, and educational penalties. Political institutions, even such clearly democratic institutions as the vote itself, are part and parcel of the network of controls which distribute resources of society in an inequitable and racist manner. Rather than being a tool available to blacks in their struggle against institutional racism, political democracy has been manipulated by white America to protect racial privilege.

It is in the arena of politics and not psychology, then, that we must look if we are to fully comprehend institutional racism, on the one hand, and black rage, on the other. Far too long have weighty theses been advanced which "psychologize away" the black citizen's anger—tracing that anger to the pathology of the ghetto rather than to the arrangements which sustain that ghetto. But what American society faces is a political crisis, a crisis brought about because the promises and practices of political democracy have never been extended below some fixed social line established by racial and economic conditions. Although one may speak of "black frustration," it is inappropriate to assume that this frustration is the product of

78

individual maladjustment; rather it is the product of political conditions and arrangements; it is an enraged reaction against white institutions and not a psychological response to blackness.

To analyze racism in American society we turn attention to the political institutions and practices which have excluded blacks from those processes which fix social goals and determine means for reaching those goals. Because the black population has never been represented proportionately to its size at any political level, the establishment of social and political priorities has failed to reflect black needs and wants. The services provided by the state have been poor, and they are deteriorating in many cases. The attempts by black citizens to change their lot have been thwarted by a wall of institutional resistance. It should come as no surprise that new forms of political expression, such as the sit-in, demonstrations, community anger and uprisings, and so forth, have appeared as alternatives to the voicelessness in the councils of power. The search for new political forms is a sign that the "normal" channels have not worked. A review of the relationship of the black community to local and national political bodies will make it abundantly clear why the old forms prevented self-determination for black citizens.

A frequently encountered argument for the flexibility of the American political system employs the analogy between European immigrant groups and the black population. It is true that there are superficial similarities between the immigrants and the blacks, but the differences which separate them—differences based on the racism of whites toward blacks—cast severe doubts on any theories of black politics that rely on the historical examples of Irish or Italian politics.

European white minorities that arrived on the American scene after the Civil War encountered a political system that on the whole excluded the moneyless and the alien from positions of political importance. However, with naturalization, the Irish, Italians, Germans, and other European groups received the vote. And on the basis of the vote, they organized, first their neighborhoods and communities and subsequently as national groups, with the help of labor organizations. Voting as blocs, especially in the large cities, the immigrant groups exchanged their vote for tolerance and patronage from the established centers of power. Soon the local ethnic associations were able to nominate and elect candidates of their own, and the immigrant communities gradually assumed some control over their own lives.

Racial practices and prejudices have prevented the black masses from equaling the performance of the European aliens. It took a civil war before even the question of freedom from chattel slavery, let alone citizenship and political power, could be answered favorably for the blacks. But the Civil War, which "freed" the slave, left untouched the issue of racism. Neither land, education, nor even the nominal rights of citizenship were granted the Negro. The Compromise of 1877, ending an already weakened Reconstruction, permitted white supremacy to become the dominant form of government in the South. Jim Crow laws and the Ku Klux Klan effectively disenfranchised "citizens" just as they began to exert their independence. The record of the North was hardly an improvement; there was, as today, a notable lack of enthusiasm for citizen rights for blacks. (Only two northern states, neither of which had a large black population, voluntarily granted the suffrage to black people in the postwar period.)

Within the black community, the power brokers were either white or were blacks used by whites to keep the black masses isolated from politics. Booker T. Washington's philosophy dominated: it was not important for black people to function as a political bloc; rather they were to cultivate the virtues of humility and subservience until such time as the white man saw fit to admit them to the spheres of political power.

This doctrine of silence and patient long-suffering was based on the hard fact that the Civil War did not alter the white citizen's determination to exclude the black population from political life. There was no naturalization process for the "freed" slave, no citizenship education in public schools, and no granting of political power, not even the right to vote.

Furthermore, whereas the immigrant laborers were able to find temporary allies in other alien groups and other parts of the working class, black people have never been able to find allies in this society. Any white faction, no matter how oppressed itself, prefers to think of black people as beneath them and thus as not meriting membership in any alliance with common economic or political grievances.

Race has created a barrier to political participation and power that is much more difficult to surmount than was the gap between Anglo-Saxons and the Irish or Italians. Just as the authors of the Constitution did not extend the right of citizenship to the slaves, so have American leaders since the founding of the country refused to recognize black people as political beings with a right to share in the domestic balance of power.

In the era that opened with the Supreme Court decision of 1954, declaring segregated schools unconstitutional, new attention has been focused on the relationship of black people to politics and law. However, the net result of a series of civil rights laws and court decisions has been a rise in expectations within the black community but little or no increase in their representation in the law-making bodies. Beneath the veneer of federal concern there lies a massive intransigence to black participation at all levels of the political structure. The fundamental power of the vote for black people has either been flatly denied or emasculated through political maneuvers. Local government is gravitating toward at-large rule by the white majority with virtually no black representation. The national government is plagued by the party kingmakers and the antiquated system of congressional committees, which are notable for their outright opposition to meaningful black participation.

DENIED THE VOTE

For the last few decades Americans concerned with establishing Constitutional rights for all citizens have been aware of the forms of black disenfranchisement practiced in the South. The clear injustices of "poll taxes" and "literacy tests" and "Constitution tests" and "Grandfather clauses" have been exposed and condemned by the liberal faction of the nation. The federal government responded to the exposure—under considerable pressure—by outlawing the unnecessary requirements for voter registration. Federal courts were empowered to appoint referees who could step into a situation in which local registrars exhibited a definite pattern of discrimination.

But despite the fact that the Justice Department and the courts have eliminated blatant forms of discrimination in voter registration, black people continue to be grossly underrepresented. In the South, white supremacists have found subtler ways of keeping blacks off voter lists. Some offices manage to slow down the registration process by feigning ineptitude, thereby registering only a handful of people while hundreds wait outside in line. Particularly in rural areas and small towns, the fear of white violence and economic reprisals continues to keep many black people away from the polls. Ghetto residents, usually a part of the menial labor force, find it difficult to spend much time studying the political situation. Ill health, malnutrition, and the disease of despair work to keep black people in all parts of the country away from the polling place and the town meeting. There is a justifiable cynicism rampant in the ghetto that discourages optimism about voting one's way out of oppression and poverty.

In those cities where substantial numbers of black people vote, a variety of institutional arrangements dilute the power of bloc voting. Perhaps the most familiar practice is known as gerrymandering; that is, the redrawing of district lines in order to lessen the power base that a black community has because of its vote. If the voting population of a city is a third black, it does not follow that a third of the city council will be directly responsive to the demands of the ghetto. The black population can be carved up and placed in voting districts in a manner that gives whites a majority in every district. "New York's 16 per cent Negro population elects only one of the city's nineteen Congressmen (Powell), two of the thirty-seven city councilmen." [1] New York is not an isolated example. In Los Angeles, "most elective constituencies are districted in a way that dilutes Negro and Mexican-American power at the polls." [2]

---

[1] *Time*, October 28, 1966, p. 33.

[2] David Sears, *Los Angeles Riot Study, Political Attitudes of Los Angeles Negroes*, Institute of Government and Public Affairs, UCLA, pp. 5–6.

"In some ways, Los Angeles' political institutions would seem to be uniquely structured to minimize the voice of Negroes in their own

Studies on Detroit, Chicago and other large cities show similar results. Congress has between 1 and 2 per cent blacks among its members while black people comprise 11 per cent of the national population. Lack of proportional representation is a nationwide phenomenon for black people.

Gerrymandering is not limited to urban centers. The black community of East Palo Alto, California, when combined with the neighboring black community of East Menlo Park, forms a sizable voting bloc in any Congressional election. East Menlo Park contains much white-owned and white-run industry and is therefore a good tax base. The area was annexed into the city of Menlo Park and so provided that community with additional tax revenue. East Palo Alto has no taxable industry and is clearly an unprofitable area in terms of annexation; hence, Menlo Park has chosen to exclude the people of East Palo Alto from its city boundaries. The two black communities were also divided by Congressional redistricting. East Palo Alto was included in a Congressional district which lies on the *other side of San Francisco Bay*. The black people of these two communities have had their voting power drastically reduced by the maneuvers of annexation and redistricting. One of the communities has become the victim of direct white economic exploitation (certainly nothing new to black communities), the other has been politically isolated, and both have been denied the power their vote would have if they were united.

THE CRISIS IN LOCAL GOVERNMENT

The immigrant minorities depended on the machine-boss style of politics to secure for themselves a niche in the power structure of the city. This system allowed every neighborhood and ethnic minor-

---

affairs. Unlike many Eastern cities, Los Angeles covers a large geographic area, and incorporates many 'bedroom suburbs' that elsewhere are separate municipalities. The white middle-class, rather than the black lower-class, represents a vast voting majority. (Negroes accounted for 13.5% of the Los Angeles population in 1960.) And most elective constituencies are districted in a way that dilutes Negro and Mexican-American power at the polls."

ity to have at least a single voice in the city council, and the local
alderman was a familiar figure to much of the population of his
ward. However, as the party organization became entrenched, it
tended to lose much of its representative quality and to rely solely
on the power of patronage jobs to sustain itself. In core-city areas
that became populated by black people, the party machine would
buy off the best of the leadership and entrench their control through
the use of the patronage system. The black population, with its
unique need for a political voice which could be used against the
exploiters of its neighborhoods, was inadequately represented in
machine politics. But at least there was some sense of identification
with the political power structure of the city.

Reform politics has not been the boon to the black community
that many would suppose. The new nonpartisan politics of the cities
emphasizes efficiency and neutrality of officials. Local leaders should
be technocrats rather than politicians, according to this theory. Consequently city government has become highly professionalized and
unresponsive to the opinions of minorities of all types. Lane states:

> Municipal reforms of this nature: nonpartisanship, smaller city
> councils, the replacement of mayors by city-managers, may serve
> admirable technical purposes and in the long run be in the best
> interests of most groups in the community—but they weaken the
> political ties of the disorganized and depressed groups in the com-
> munity. And, in doing this, they serve a strong, but usually re-
> pressed, interest of the community "power elite," whose focus is
> ostensibly upon the gains in efficiency and honesty brought about
> by the reforms, but who profit from the political apathy of the
> underdog.[3]

In the old politics an ethnic or religious minority could control
its own ward and be assured of at least one representative in the
ruling body. In the new city, the trend is toward at-large elections,
which benefit only the groups that hold a majority in the entire city.

> Other things being equal, Negro political strength in the city
> organizations tends to be directly proportional to the size and

[3] Robert E. Lane, *Political Life* (New York: The Free Press of Glencoe, 1960), pp. 270–71.

density of the Negro population and inversely proportional to the
size of the basic political unit.[4]

A similar dilemma awaits our metropolitan centers in the near
future as the pressure mounts for government structures that will
include suburbs as well as the urban centers. The arguments for
regional planning are strong. Taxable capital is moving out of the
city and into the white suburbs, but the money is desperately
needed to meet the social problems of the inner city. The funds will
be welcomed by city governments that are increasingly feeling the
pinch caused by the exodus of industry and the influx of the poor.
But the money will inevitably create a demand among suburbanites
that they have a say in its use. Just as black people are approaching
the point where they could seize a large share of power in city
government, they may find themselves faced with a regional government over which they have little or no control.

Liberal whites argue that events such as the elections of Stokes
and Hatcher to the mayorships of Cleveland and Gary show that
black people are gradually arriving at their rightful place in the
political process. The Stokes and Hatcher elections were significant
in that both men relied heavily on solid ghetto support for their
victories. Big city elections will become easier for black candidates
to win as the black population passes 50 per cent. But black
people can never hope to approach a voting majority in most electoral districts, although they will continue to constitute a significant
minority. Most black candidates for office will still have to appeal to
a large segment of the white community if they hope to be elected.
Thus, although a small number of cases where black people have
been elected to political positions do exist, a great majority of these
black leaders fail to effect desperately needed social change. In
terms of strict definition, the black man may be represented, but in
terms of actual political power, he is still a second-class citizen.

In machine politics the black politician had to conform to the
rules of the game as they were set by the white bosses. In the new,
nonpartisan style of governing, the black leader must compromise

[4] James Q. Wilson, *Negro Politics* (New York: The Free Press of Glencoe, 1960), p. 27.

the demands of his people to appeal to large blocs of white voters. In either case, the process of "co-optation" cripples black representation in government. For the purposes of this study, "co-optation" can be defined as the process whereby individuals are assimilated and committed to the institutions and the values of the dominant group in the society. The dominant group in our society is, of course, white. This holds true whether one accepts the "pluralist" model of society, in which power resides in a number of focal points, or the "elite" model, which suggests a unified "power elite." As Carmichael and Hamilton point out,

> American pluralism quickly becomes a monolithic structure on issues of race. When faced with demands from black people, the multi-faction whites unite and present a common front.[5]

What does co-optation mean to the black who wants and needs his leaders to push for social reform? A specific example will illustrate that in order for blacks to attain positions of power, they must "sell-out"—accept and espouse the goals and ideals of the established power group. In 1939, William L. Dawson, a black member of the City Council in Chicago, a militant, and a Republican, switched parties with the full backing of the Democratic machine that controls Chicago politics. As James Q. Wilson points out in his book, *Negro Politics*:

> Dawson, before being co-opted into the Democratic Party, was an outspoken and vigorous champion of racial causes. Once inside an organization that was strong and which manifestly held the key to the future, race matters were subdued.[6]

Wilson further states:

> . . . the civic issues which the Negro protest and improvement associations define as important—open occupancy, fair employment practices, medical integration—are not common topics in the politicians' contacts with the voters.[7]

As young organizations value change, so mature organizations value order, and the leading Negro politicians have so completely moved

---

[5] Stokely Carmichael and Charles V. Hamilton, *Black Power: The Politics of Liberation in America* (New York: Vintage Books, 1967), p. 7.
[6] Wilson, p. 36.
[7] *Ibid.*, p. 54.

from youthful change to present order that their aversion to issues, publicity, and protest action has smothered all sense of the urgent need to press the demands of the ghetto on the public. The co-optation of his leader into the dominant power group left the black man in Chicago with a figurehead leader and no one in power to push for needed legislation.

NATIONAL POLITICS: THE PRIVATE CLUB

The two major political parties, which afford citizens the one means for controlling national government, present major road-blocks to black participation.

American parties exemplify American social values, or perhaps respond to them, by their broad electoral appeals and notably by their leaderships. These leaderships have always been heavily middle-class, including some who entered the middle-class after upward mobility, educationally and occupationally, from working-class families. At no time have American party leaders been recruited in significant numbers directly from working-class ranks.[8]

Thus, black people, who are working-class or unemployed, are not now, nor will they be in the foreseeable future, empowered in any substantial manner. Parties both reflect and reinforce the political culture of a given system, and the political culture of our system has long been a major force in subjugating the black by such mechanisms as exclusion, nonenforcement of the laws, and co-optation. In fact, every black is co-opted into the system insofar as he gives his vote to candidates who will not or cannot work for the things that the black man needs. The party system is unwilling and unable to change fast enough to satisfy the need for black political participation.

. . . parties, once started in a certain mold, are likely to persist in that mold even after the original conditioning circumstances have

[8] Leon Epstein, "Political Parties in Western Democratic Systems," in *Political Parties,* ed. Roy Macridis (New York: Harper and Row, 1967), p. 139.

changed considerably. The parties too, it is appreciated, can and do change, but slowly and not in all respects.[9]

The Democratic Party, which most black people follow, was begun long before blacks were at all involved in politics. The structures and institutions in the party are not arranged to include blacks in power-broker positions. The party bosses have become so entrenched that a group hoping to enter the party today cannot expect a fair share of control.

Exclusiveness in the Democratic Party can best be illustrated in the delegate selection process preceding the national convention. In forty of the fifty states, delegates are chosen, not by election, but rather by either the state convention or the state committee.[10] For example, in Georgia,

> The Democratic Party rules designate the chairman of the State Democratic Executive Committee as a delegate to the National Convention and provide that all other delegates, alternates and vacancies shall be designated by the Chairman of the State Democratic Executive Committee with the advice and consent of the Democratic Gubernatorial Nominee.[11]

This type of arrangement exists in most Southern states, but it is not exclusive to that area. New York and South Dakota also select their delegates by the state committee method. Even in states where the delegates are elected to the state conventions, the chairman or the executive committee wields power, for he or they, as the case may be, has the power to determine how many delegates each district will send to the state convention.[12]

Racism is allowed to flourish in this type of system in two ways. In the case of Georgia and other Southern states, where those in the powerful positions are overt and individual racists, they can effectively exclude all blacks from the delegation. But even in the liberal north, racism excludes blacks from such positions. Delegates are

[9] Ibid., p. 139.
[10] Nomination and Election of the President and Vice-President of the United States Including the Manner of Selecting Delegates to National Political Conventions, compiled by Frances Valeo, U.S. Government Printing Office, 1968, pp. 61–65.
[11] Ibid., p. 85.
[12] Ibid., pp. 65–156.

appointed largely in terms of how much money they have contributed to the party and how much standing they have in the community. In other words, political patronage determines who will serve, and poor people, therefore blacks, are denied access.

Not only are black people excluded from the selection of delegates to the national convention, but also the few who do manage to become delegates are effectively prevented from voicing any serious complaints on the race question by the rules that govern the convention and its national committee. The rules permit the national committee, a group consisting of one man and one woman from each state and territory, to run the convention with an almost absolute authority.[13]

The Mississippi Freedom Democratic Party (MFDP) provides an example of the experiences that have made black political activists aware of the difficulty in gaining the power within the major parties that might be expected to accompany their voting strength. The MFDP was organized in 1964 with the objective of being recognized by the national party as the official Democratic party in the state. The MFDP stressed four main points at the convention:

1. It was an open political party. It excluded no one because of race, creed, or color.

[13] For example, article 4, paragraph 2, of the rules governing the committee says, "Contests as to the membership on the National Committee referred by the National Convention to the incoming National Committee shall be heard and adjudicated by the National Committee." The body is, in other words, a self-perpetuating group, and if someone feels that he has a just complaint about its membership, he must take his case to the very group he wishes to challenge! Furthermore, article 7, paragraph 3 states, "Upon the written petition of thirty (30) or more members of the National Committee, filed with the chairman concurrently or separately within a period of thirty (30) days, it shall be the duty of the chairman within fifteen (15) days from receipt of such petition or petitions to issue a call for a meeting of the National Committee, to be held in Washington, D.C., or such city as may be indicated in such petitions or such petition to be the common choice of not less than thirty (30) members of said National Committee." Obviously poor people cannot afford to take time off from work to fly to Washington or some other city for such a meeting. The ghetto is excluded even further, therefore, because the only black people who could afford such a luxury are those "Negroes" who have long since left the ghetto for the middle-class suburbs.

2. It supported the platform of the National Democratic Party. On June 30, 1964, the "regular" party had rejected the national party platform.

3. It was willing to sign the oath to remain loyal to the national party. Only four out of sixty-eight "regulars" signed such a pledge.

4. It supported and would actively campaign for the national Democratic candidates. The "regular" delegates did not; in fact, they later campaigned for the Republican candidates and helped to deliver that state to Goldwater in November, 1964.[14]

By the time the convention opened, the MFDP had the written support of nine northern states (who stood to gain if southern Senators could be removed and thus the chairmanships of important committees opened), the United Auto Workers, and the Americans for Democratic Action. Pressure from the Administration caused *all* the MFDP backers to withdraw. The national party then upheld the "regular" party, which had passed a resolution on July 28, 1964,

[14] "The major counter-charge presented by the 'regulars' was that the MFDP delegates were chosen illegally; that the precinct, county, and state conventions they held were 'outside the law.' This was ludicrous at best, because the 'regular' state party had been choosing delegates illegally for years, even to the extent of excluding not only blacks but many whites. The 'regular' state party made no pretense of holding open, local county conventions. When Mississippi blacks attempted to attend the precinct and county meetings of the 'regular' party, it was often impossible for them even to locate the meeting place. In 8 precincts in 6 different counties, MFDP representatives went to polling stations at the time designated for the meeting but were unable to find any evidence of a meeting. Some officials denied knowledge of such a gathering; others claimed the meeting had already been held. In 6 different counties where meetings were held, MFDP people were refused entrance. In the town of Hattiesburg, the black people were told that they could not participate without showing poll tax receipts, despite a recent Constitutional amendment outlawing such a requirement. In 10 precincts of 5 different counties, black Mississippians were allowed to attend but their participation was restricted: some were not allowed to vote, others were not permitted to nominate delegates from the floor. The MFDP, on the other hand, held open conventions and excluded no one. They abided by the law *legally;* they did not control the law *politically.*" Carmichael and Hamilton, pp. 90–91.

saying, in part, "We believe in separation of the races in all phases of our society." [15]

> Many labor, liberal, and civil rights leaders deserted the MFDP because of closer ties to the national Democratic party. To seat the MFDP over the "regulars" would have meant a displacement of power, and it became crystal clear that in order to combat power, one needed power. Black people would have to organize and obtain their own power base before they could begin to think of coalition with others. To rely on the absolute existence of external, liberal, labor forces was not a wise procedure.[16]

Within the Congress there are a number of serious obstacles in the way of black political power, and even whites seeking to support the demands of the black community find it very difficult to overcome the intransigence and inertia of a committee system based on seniority. Power in Congress accrues to those who can be elected regularly with a minimum of effort—in other words, Democrats from the one-party states of the South and Republicans from the rural Midwest. Assignment to desired committee seats, attainment of coveted committee chairmanships, the norms of respect and deference, all favor the member who can be consistently reelected.

Of the 122 Democratic "safe" seats in the House of Representatives, 77 are in the South, mostly in rural areas. Most of the Republican safe seats are in the Midwest farm regions. Black people are not represented in either area. There are simply no black people in the rural Midwest, and most southern Congressmen are elected precisely because they are actively opposed to any legislation aiding black people. The continued registration of black voters may change this. However, even if blacks can exercise a "swing" vote, changes in public policy are not necessarily certain. Northern blacks have had the vote for many years.

White southerners are preoccupied with a single issue: race. Those districts where blacks do have significant influence with their Congressman, because they can provide the margin of support in a close election, are two-party districts, and any candidate

[15] *Ibid.*, p. 93.
[16] *Ibid.*, p. 96.

representing one will probably lose fairly often and so will probably not be able to build up much seniority.

Both the House and the Senate are organized around their committees. There are twenty in the House, sixteen in the Senate. The work of shaping bills, investigating their effects, and working out compromises occurs in committee. A bill must obtain committee support to pass Congress. If a bill is pigeonholed or killed outright in committee, there is virtually no chance that it will pass either house. The committee is almost totally responsible for this final shape of the bill, and few substantive changes are made once the bill has been reported to the rest of the House.

The manner of assigning Congressmen to committees favors those who have seniority and who most consent to the status quo. In the Senate, assignments of Democrats to committees are made by the party's Steering Committee, along with the majority leader. Until 1965, seven out of fifteen members of the Steering Committee were from the South, and two others, Hayden of Arizona and Bible of Nevada, were extremely conservative. Only four were from northern industrial states. Two liberal Democrats were then added, and the committee was increased to seventeen members—with the Southerners and conservatives still holding nine places.

In the House, Democratic assignments are made by the Democratic members of the Ways and Means Committee, chaired by Wilbur Mills of Arkansas. Ways and Means consists of mostly senior congressmen from safe districts, not responsive to electoral changes and public opinion trends. It is like a firmly entrenched bureaucracy. Each man on the committee is responsible for a "zone" of states. For a Congressman to be considered for a committee position, he must be nominated by his zone man. Although the zone man will almost always do this if asked, it is not always done enthusiastically—and this "veto by silence" will block Representatives unacceptable to those in power.

Since nine of the sixteen Senate chairmanships and twelve of the twenty in the House are held by Southerners, the South exercises an important influence on the ideological composition of committees, and the basic unity of the party's membership on committees tends to be maintained. A candidate who attacks the status quo—especially one who strikes at the entrenched powers of the committees through attacks on seniority and on rules—can be punished by being passed over by the majority of conservatives sitting on the bodies that determine committee membership. Thus, those few northern liberals who do attempt to speak for black people are constrained by the almost insurmountable institutionalization of structures and systems in Congress which have clearly racist effects.

THE REORDERING OF POWER RELATIONSHIPS

The ghetto communities are becoming increasingly organized to demand changes in inner-city conditions and to take control of programs that directly affect their lives. These new groups must of necessity come up against the old, unresponsive power structures. The critical question for American politics and ultimately for the national destiny is whether or not new forms can evolve which will provide for a large measure of black control of black communities and their resources. If dramatic structural changes are not forthcoming, the racial crisis is bound to deepen even if relief and employment programs are improved. Black people wish to create their own future and not simply be spoon fed by a hand that could be withdrawn overnight.

The War on Poverty, as confusing and as stop-gap as it was, contained one concept that for a time promised to bring important changes in the distribution of power. This was the Community Action Program, which called for the formation of Councils in target areas to oversee the OEO programs in that area. These Councils were to be so composed that they achieved "maximum feasible participation" of the poor. According to John Donovan, the consequences of CAP were not well understood by most members of the Johnson administration. "Community action involved the use of federal funds to exert pressure on local bureaucracies, to encourage them to innovate and challenge them to create new institutions." [17]

The Community Action Councils were potential centers of political power and representation for the people of the ghettos. It did

[17] John Donovan, *The Politics of Poverty* (New York: Pegasus, 1967), pp. 39–41.

not take long for the city governments to realize the threat to their control that CAP created in inner-city neighborhoods.

> From the beginning of the Community Action Programs, it was clear to any alert politician that "community action" and "citizen participation" imply direct confrontation with established systems of political power and social control. To create new organizations that control money and jobs and that operate programs that directly affect people in the street, is to create new bases for political power. The easiest way to prevent this is to have the old systems run the new programs: and this is the pattern that pervades CAP around the nation.[18]

The local councils in most cases have been packed with members hand picked by city hall, or new structures have been created to bypass the community councils. The larger and more powerful the city organization, the less likely it was that OEO would allow CAP to come into conflict with the local government.

Although the CAP attempt at community organization has been largely crushed by the political power of the old guard, the experience has indicated what direction city politics must take in the next decade. The black community will continue to organize *outside* the established systems. To do this the black leadership will need funds from sources that are more independent than the federal government. It will also need pressure from white individuals and groups on city and county governments to force open the structures to allow for "maximum feasible participation" of black people in the control of their own destinies.

Black people are *not* talking about a coalition of white and black liberals that could try to talk the federal and local governments into better relief programs. The black community must build within itself the power to control. Carmichael and Hamilton articulated this new strategy:

> It is absolutely imperative that black people strive to form an independent base of political power *first*. When they can control their own communities—however large or small—then other groups

[18] David Stoloff, "Poverty and Welfare," in *The Great Society Reader: The Failure of American Liberalism*, eds. Marvin E. Gettleman and David Mermelstein (New York: Vintage Books, 1967), pp. 236–37.

will make overtures to them based on a wise calculation of self-interest. The blacks will have the mobilized ability to grant or withhold from coalition. Black people must set about to build those new forms of politics.[19]

New political forms are emerging to give expression to black unity. These new organizations and parties will grow increasingly separated from the white community *unless* significant pressure develops in some segment of white society to remove the roadblocks in the way of black power. The major obstacles, as we have seen, are obstruction or dilution of the power of the vote; remote, white-controlled local government; and an antiquated federal system.

Perhaps the most significant fact about these problems is that in many ways, the white community is also suffering from their effects. Of course, one can never compare lack of white participation to the almost total exclusion of black people; but there are grievances of a parallel nature. Black people are not the only ones who have taken to the streets and to the picket lines. White students and even suburban housewives have felt the need for new means of political power, a sign that the present arrangements are inadequate to meet the felt need for expression.

[19] Carmichael and Hamilton, p. 96.

Chapter 7

Why White Americans Are Healthier

In its preamble, the World Health Organization recognizes health as a state of complete physical, mental, and social well-being and not merely the absence of disease or infirmity. Many institutions in a society, therefore, influence the health of members of that society. Nevertheless, there are specific institutions which have the overall responsibility for the prevention of disease and maintenance of health in the population. These health institutions deal primarily with the direct treatment of diseased patients. This implies in turn the social responsibility to recognize and define all causes of disease and disability and then to mobilize the medical and social resources needed to combat those causes. Since the responsibility of the health institutions is so comprehensive, if it is shown that the level of health of some racially distinct group is markedly inferior, this situation would have to be called in part a racist consequence of the actions and structures of those health institutions.

By almost all measures, such a situation does exist in this country: the health of black people in the United States is vastly inferior to that of whites. Let us first consider one of the most basic indicators —general mortality rates. A recent summary by the U.S. Department of Health, Education, and Welfare clearly shows the difference in white and nonwhite mortality rates (black people comprised 92 per cent of the nonwhite population sampled). Age-specific death rates calculated from these 1963 statistics proved to be higher for blacks than for whites for all ages below 75. In the prime 25–44 age group, black mortality was over twice that of whites, as shown in Table I.

TABLE I [1]

1963 AGE-SPECIFIC DEATH RATES

(Rate per 1,000 Population in Each Age Group)

Age	White	Nonwhite
Under 1	22.3	41.7
1–4	0.9	1.8
5–14	0.4	0.6
15–24	1.0	1.6
25–34	1.3	3.2
35–44	2.6	6.5
45–54	6.8	13.2
55–64	16.2	27.9
65–74	37.5	52.9
75–84	85.8	74.9
85+	215.8	145.7
All ages	9.5	10.1

Although the overall differential mortality for all ages appears small, this is somewhat deceiving since the nonwhite population is much younger than the white one. That is, a greater percentage of the total nonwhite population is found in age-groups which for whites are associated with lower mortality. When corrected for this factor, the overall age-specific nonwhite mortality rate was actually 47 per cent greater than the white rate in 1963.[2]

Other more specific mortality rates also indicate that American health institutions do not meet the needs of black people as well as they meet the needs of whites. Maternal mortality, for example, is four times higher for blacks than for whites; and infant mortality is also greater for blacks, as shown in Table II.

Similarly, the mortality rates for most specific diseases were higher for black people, as shown in Table III, which also indicates the interesting fact that the differential is highest for the infectious

[1] Helen C. Chase, "White-Nonwhite Mortality Differentials in the United States," in *Health, Education, and Welfare Indicators*, U.S. Dept. of Health, Education, and Welfare, June, 1965, p. 29.
[2] *Ibid.*

TABLE II [3]

1965 MATERNITY AND INFANT MORTALITY RATES

	White	Nonwhite
Maternal deaths/100,000 live births	21.0	83.7
Infant deaths/1,000 live births:		
0–28 days old	16.1	24.7
28 days–one year old	5.4	14.6

disease group. By and large, medical science has not made a dramatic reduction in mortality due to malignant disease even in the white community, so that lack of medical care does not affect the course of these diseases markedly from one racial group to the next. Medical science has, however, found cures and controls for most infectious diseases, which have greatly reduced their mortality rates in the white community. But the health institutions have failed to effectively extend this significant medical progress to the black community. This failure for health improvement to be equal in both the white and black communities is well noted in the specific example of Watts, where a 1960 survey revealed that though Watts accounted for only 17 per cent of Los Angeles' population, Watts

TABLE III [4]

AGE-SPECIFIC MORTALITY RATES FOR VARIOUS DISEASES

(Deaths/100,000 Population in 1963)

	White	Nonwhite	Ratio: Nonwhite to White
Selected infectious diseases:			
Tuberculosis	3.4	12.8	3.8
Syphilis	0.9	4.3	4.8
Dysentery	0.1	0.5	5.0
Influenza and pneumonia	24.4	55.4	2.3
Cardio-vascular-renal diseases	380.1	521.8	1.4
Malignant tumors	123.7	145.2	1.2

[3] U.S. Dept. of Commerce, *Statistical Abstracts of the United States,* 88th edition, 1967, p. 56.

[4] Chase, p. 31.

had 100 per cent of Los Angeles' cases of polio, 100 per cent of the diphtheria, as well as a disproportionate percentage of many other diseases.[5]

In summary, the health institutions in this country have not eliminated the following racial distribution of health: in 1965, white males at birth enjoyed a life expectancy 6.5 years longer than did black males (67.7 vs. 61.1) while white females enjoyed an extra 7.3 years (74.7 vs. 67.4).[6] It thus seems clear that the institutions charged with promoting the health of all Americans have not done their job equally well for all population groups, to the special detriment of black people in America. Granted this, one must now ask if the disparity between white and black levels of health is at least decreasing in any discernible degree.

To answer this question, we must distinguish between improving health, on the one hand, and decreasing disparity between black and white health, on the other. There is no question that the health of all Americans—black and white—has improved over the years. The overall mortality in 1900 was 17.0/1,000 population for whites and 25.0 for nonwhites, whereas the figures in 1963 (uncorrected for age, as noted above) were 9.5 and 10.1 respectively.[7] But the relevant question is: Are blacks benefiting from health progress as much as whites are? Are the health institutions making sure that blacks are catching up to white levels of health? There are two ways of looking at this. First, one can simply look at the ratio of black mortality rates to the counterpart white rate at various points in time. These are arrayed in Table IV.

The data for maternal and infant mortality show that the gap has widened considerably for the last twenty years, and there is no significant indication that the trend is changing. The tuberculosis and pneumonia data show that while the gap has not widened, there has been no progress toward narrowing the gap over the years.

Second, let us consider the time-lag statistic suggested by Rashi

---

[5] Cited in "A University of Southern California Proposal for Development and Operation of the Family Neighborhood Health Services Center" for Watts, University of Southern California, 1966.

[6] *Statistical Abstracts*, p. 55.

[7] Chase, p. 28.

TABLE IV

RATIO OF NONWHITE TO WHITE MORTALITY FOR SELECTED GROUPS AND DISEASES

	1930	1940	1950	1960	1963	1964	1965
Maternal mortality/ 100,000 live births:[8]							
Nonwhite		773.50	221.60	97.90		89.90	83.70
White		319.80	61.10	26.00		22.30	21.00
Ratio		2.42	3.63	3.89		4.02	3.99
Infant mortality (deaths in first year/1,000 live births):[9]							
Nonwhite		73.80	44.50	43.30		41.10	40.30
White		43.20	26.80	22.90		21.60	21.50
Ratio		1.71	1.66	1.90		1.90	1.85
Deaths due to tuberculosis/ 100,000 population:[10]							
Nonwhite	199.40	132.90	67.50	15.10	12.80		
White	60.60	36.10	16.60	4.40	3.40		
Ratio	3.30	3.68	4.06	3.44	3.87		
Deaths due to pneumonia and influenza/ 100,000 population:[11]							
Nonwhite	194.30	138.10	56.90	55.20	55.40		
White	99.10	63.00	22.90	25.60	24.40		
Ratio	1.94	2.19	2.48	2.24	2.27		

Fein. What Fein notes is that it took white America a certain number of years to make the scientific and organizational discoveries needed to improve its health as judged, say, by life expectancy. Once the knowledge on how to do this was available, however, it should have been possible to make the same improvement in life expectancy for black America in less time, since the scientific advance was already made. Is this in fact the case? For example,

In 1900, white male life expectancy at birth was 48.2 years—by 1940 it was 62.8 years—a gain of 15 years in four decades. But for

[8] *Statistical Abstracts*, p. 56.
[9] *Ibid.*
[10] Chase, p. 31.
[11] *Ibid.*

the Negro, too, a full forty years were needed to progress over the same range: from 47.1 years in 1920 to 61.5 years in 1960.[12]

In other words, blacks were not profiting by the earlier advances; they did not glean the benefits of technological acceleration as they would have if racist barriers did not exist.

On the basis of the foregoing information, it seems necessary to conclude that American health institutions are racist and the extent of this racism is not decreasing. This racism seems a powerful indictment of a system of medical care which (1) is capable of offering part of its population the best health care in the world, but (2) has the ultimate responsibility for providing health care for everyone in a country that believes all men have certain inalienable rights to life. How do the American health institutions contribute to this racist situation? What has allowed fact and philosophy to become so disparate? Is the answer within the system of distribution of medical care itself, or is it in the failure of the nation's institutions to insure an equitable distribution of social progress and social justice in general? It is difficult to answer these questions, for two main reasons. First, there is no uniform system of health care to analyze, but rather a very complex series of independent institutions which must act together to provide health care. No single official governing body has had ultimate responsibility and power for health planning. Second, in contrast to some other institutions in this country, there is as yet very little systematic data available on the racial composition and racial consequences of actions taken by the American health institutions. In fact, this lack of self-analysis (and the apparent self-satisfaction that it betrays) seems to be one of the most telling features of this "system" of health institutions. If they are concerned with actually improving the health of all people, it would seem that a much greater research effort ought to be directed toward ways in which health is distributed and how it can be better distributed, lest the advances made by the laboratory research efforts remain available only to privileged segments of the society. It is noteworthy that much of

[12] Rashi Fein, "An Economic and Social Profile of the Negro American," *Daedalus*, Fall 1965, p. 820.

the available pertinent data has been collected by civil rights organizations and not by the health institutions at all. Despite the inadequacy of the data, there are features of the current institutional structure which can be discussed—the method of distribution of services, the racial aspects of various components of the health care system such as physicians and their organization, and hospitals and their practices.

One important way in which mortality is reduced is through contact with personal preventive and curative medical services. Perhaps the most striking feature of the American system of distributing these services is that except for the federally supported care for veterans and military personnel there are basically two health care systems—one for those patients who pay for these services themselves (either directly or through purchased insurance) and one for those patients who receive services paid for by public financing mechanisms. Thus, though in theory no citizen need go without care, this economic division of health services has resulted in two separate and definitely unequal levels of care, and the inequality is especially discriminatory against black people.

It is very well known that the poor Americans who participate in the health care system for the medically indigent suffer from both inferior health and inferior health care. In New York City, in 1963, the sixteen poverty areas as a group suffered an infant mortality rate 1.6 times as high as that of the rest of the city; maternal mortality was 2.4 times as high; the percentage of mothers receiving late or no prenatal care was 2.8 times as high; and the mortality for tuberculosis and pneumonia was also disproportionately high (see Table V).

And in the same city, routine immunization was shown to be much less adequate for poor people (see Table VI). It is apparent that although the purely medical aspects of care offered at centers treating the medically indigent is usually medically acceptable, the care is neither continuous nor comprehensive and the circumstances in which it is administered are generally so impersonal as to discourage even the most health-conscious individual. Too often the location of the public services, the availability of public transportation, the hours when services are offered, and so on, reflect arrange-

TABLE V [13]

HEALTH AND SOCIAL PROBLEMS IN NEW YORK POVERTY AREAS,
1963

Problem	Sixteen Poverty Areas	Rest of City	Ratio
Infant deaths/1,000 live births	34.8	21.8	1.60
Maternal mortality/100,000 births	11.8	5.0	2.36
Percentage of mothers receiving late or no prenatal care	38.4	14.0	2.74
Crude death rate/100,000 population:			
Tuberculosis	15.3	6.9	2.21
Diabetes	23.4	22.3	1.05
Pneumonia and influenza	53.5	41.0	1.30
Home accidents	13.7	11.8	1.16

ments which are convenient for the providers of service but inconvenient for the patients. And the patient who is persistent enough to arrive at the clinic at the proper time must all too often face long waits in dingy surroundings, only to then have to describe his

TABLE VI [14]

FULL IMMUNIZATION OF CHILDREN ONE TO FOUR YEARS OF AGE
ACCORDING TO FAMILY INCOME AND TYPE OF IMMUNIZATION,
New York, 1964

	Percentage Fully Immunized		
Family Income	Diphtheria, Pertussis, and Tetanus	Polio	Smallpox
0–$1,999	50.7	23.9	44.8
$2,000–$3,999	64.5	40.1	69.1
$4,000–$5,999	77.7	55.4	85.1
$6,000–$7,999	82.5	63.1	87.8
$8,000 or more	90.6	66.0	92.6

[13] Cited in Lawrence Bergner and Alonzo Yerby, "Low Income and Barriers to Use of Health Services," *New England Journal of Medicine*, CCLXXVIII, No. 10 (1968), 542.

[14] *Ibid.*, p. 542.

problem not in his own terms but in terms acceptable to the middle-class white professional.[15]

Though all poor Americans must face these obstacles to adequate health care, the fact is that they work to the particular disadvantage of black people. To begin with, black people constitute a disproportionately large segment of the poor, as shown in Table VII. Secondly, the information barrier which keeps many of the poor from

TABLE VII [16]

Distribution of White and Nonwhite Population By Family Income, 1963–64

Percentage of All Families in Particular Income Group

Income	White	Nonwhite
Under $2,000	9.7	30.8
$2,000–$3,999	15.5	30.1
$4,000–$6,999	34.5	26.0
$7,000–$9,999	22.4	8.0
$10,000 and over	17.9	5.1
	100.0	100.0

being aware of the existence and importance of services and utilizing services which are available (if not accessible) also works to the particular disadvantage of blacks, in part because of the poor health education received in inferior schools. Tables VIII and IX, taken from the U.S. Public Health Service's Health Interview Survey, correct for both income and age and show that not only are black people sicker than their income-matched white countrymen but they also use direct medical services less.

It is clear that to say health care is an economic not a racial issue is to overlook irrefutable evidence to the contrary. If the education, labor, and business institutions make it difficult for blacks to earn

---

[15] *Ibid.*, p. 544.

[16] Geraldine A. Gleeson, and Elijah L. White, "Disability and Medical Care Among Whites and Nonwhites in the United States," in *Health, Education and Welfare Indicators,* U.S. Dept. of Health, Education and Welfare, October, 1965, p. 2.

TABLE VIII [17]

AGE-ADJUSTED DISABILITY BY INCOME AND RACE, 1962–63

Family Income	Restricted Activity Days		Bed Disability Days		Work Days Lost by Employed	
	White	Nonwhite	White	Nonwhite	White	Nonwhite
Under $2,000	28.1	34.7	11.4	14.9	7.5	12.1
$2,000–$3,999	17.1	23.2	7.1	10.2	7.0	8.6
$4,000–$6,999	13.8	13.7	5.5	6.8	5.6	7.3
$7,000 and above	13.1	12.3	5.3	4.3	5.3	7.3

a decent living, medicine has helped perpetuate institutional racism by rationing health care according to ability to pay, by providing inadequate and inferior health care for poor people, and by failing

TABLE IX [18]

PHYSICIAN AND DENTIST VISITS BY INCOME AND RACE

(Age-Adjusted, 1962–63)

Family Income	Visits per Person per Year			
	Physician		Dentist	
	White	Nonwhite	White	Nonwhite
Under $2,000	4.6	3.5	0.9	0.6
$2,000–$3,999	4.5	3.9	0.9	0.6
$4,000–$6,999	4.5	3.7	1.5	1.3
$7,000–$9,999	4.7	3.6	1.9	1.7
$10,000 and above	5.1	4.1	2.8	2.1

to establish structures which can meet health needs in ways acceptable to all patients.[19]

If mortality statistics show that health is a racial matter in this country, and if one way this comes about is through the racial consequences of an economic policy of health-care distribution, it is possible to suggest other factors in the health-care institutions

[17] *Ibid.*, p. 4.

[18] *Ibid.*, p. 6.

[19] Though data are not sufficient yet, experts are already speculating that "the advent of Medicare and Medicaid . . . will not be sufficient to erase these inequities." Bergner and Yerby, p. 543.

which support this situation. What keeps the voice of the racial minority from being effectively heard?

To begin with, only 2 per cent of all doctors and dentists in the United States are black.[20] This means that one out of every 3,700 blacks is a doctor—compared to one doctor out of every 640 whites.[21] And the situation is not improving. There are two black medical schools in the United States and few black medical students enrolled in the other ninety-nine predominantly white colleges.[22] Although this lack of black students preparing for medical careers seems due to a lack of black applicants who meet the qualifications for admission to medical schools and the apparent lack of attraction of health careers for those blacks who would be qualified applicants,[23] several other factors are important.

The individual and institutional racial discrimination in the United States system of education makes it improbable that a black student will have completed the prerequisite college training to apply to medical school. The use of the Medical College Admissions Test (MCAT) as a criterion for admission systematically discriminates against black applicants—much as do IQ tests. According to Dietrich Reitzes in *Negroes and Medicine*, ". . . the MCAT reflects to a large extent the cultural experiences of the applicant." [24] The general knowledge questions constructed by white middle-class test designers are more difficult for blacks whose cultural experience and social perceptions will be considerably different from those of the test writers. Many medical schools now actively seek out "qualified" black students[25] and to this extent they are reducing the racism inherent in admission policies. But few schools have reduced the MCAT or college grades hurdles or altered their curricula to be more relevant to the needs of black people and perhaps thereby to be more attractive to black students.

[20] National Urban League, *Health Care and the Negro Population,* New York, 1965, p. 24.

[21] *Ibid.,* p. 25.

[22] *Ibid.,* p. 25.

[23] *Ibid.,* pp. 26–27.

[24] Dietrich Reitzes, *Negroes and Medicine* (Cambridge, Mass.: Harvard University Press, 1958), p. 15.

[25] John A. Kenney, "Medical Civil Rights," *Journal of the National Medical Association,* 55 (1963), 430–32.

The scarcity of black physicians has many implications for the distribution and quality of health care. To begin with, less than one-fourth of black patients are able to receive their medical care from black physicians, which means simply that three-fourths of black patients are treated by whites in situations which are not always conducive to satisfactory doctor-patient relationships due to conscious or unconscious mistreatment and mistrust. Also, the control of when, to whom, and how health care is to be dispersed is ultimately in the hands of the individual physician, but his control is limited and influenced by law, hospital policies, medical organizations, and the location of his practice. Since there are so few black physicians, this control lies almost exclusively in white hands. In addition, on the local level, many county medical societies still discriminate on the basis of race, although the terms used usually have to do with "qualifications." It is often difficult for a black doctor to find the necessary sponsorship of two member doctors in order to join, because he is black and all existing members are white.[26] Many county societies have scientific membership for blacks and full membership for whites,[27] so only whites attend the society's voting and social functions. In the last few years, many societies have indeed allowed their first blacks to receive full membership, but it seems to be one black in many such cases, though as usual statistics showing national patterns simply do not exist.[28]

The importance of insuring full membership has special implications: it is usually necessary to be a county society member to be on the local hospital staff (that is, be able to hospitalize patients there) and to thereby influence that hospital's policies; and it is necessary to be a county society member before one can be in the state society and then in the nationwide American Medical Association. The result is that at the AMA level, there is an inadequate black voice in the governing House of Delegates and no representa-

[26] *Ibid.*

[27] "Integration Battlefront," *Journal of the National Medical Association,* 55 (1963), 49–68.

[28] In a personal communication (February 16, 1968), Dr. Franz J. Ingelfinger (Editor of the prestigious *New England Journal of Medicine*) noted, "Documentation of any specific instance of discrimination is practically impossible."

tion on the Board of Trustees.[29] The result is that the national organization tolerates discrimination at local levels,[30] and the special health needs of the black communities are not taken into account in the planning of health services. When blacks have no voice, the organization of medical services can easily work against the legitimate interests of black physicians and patients. Fortunately, more and more black physicians are gradually—but only after much effort—being given admission to hospital staffs.[31] But this process needs to be rapidly accelerated.

Lack of black representation and control is also present in the field of preventive medicine and public health.

> The health department staff often lacks the broad spectrum of interests represented in the community . . . the health department staff tends to be drawn from middle and upper-middle economic groups and only rarely from the extremes of the socioeconomic scales. Similarly, it frequently has no representation of minority groups, either racial, religious, or political. Not only does it usually not have the benefit of members of such groups on its staff, but it often has no appreciation of the needs and desires of these groups. This lack of understanding is a concomitant of the restrictive policies, written or unwritten, which bar employment of qualified personnel for reasons of prejudice. The pursuit of such policies can then be seen to be self-defeating.[32]

A typical result of white ignorance in positions of leadership is to be found in the educational pamphlets written for ghetto residents by white middle-class professionals in middle-class terms which are nearly incomprehensible to the people who are supposed to learn from them.[33]

[29] "The Board of Trustees, Members of the House of Delegates," *Journal of the American Medical Association*, 204 (1968), 455–60.

[30] "Equal Rights, Privileges, and Responsibilities," editorial, *New England Journal of Medicine*, 278 (1968), 215–16.

[31] For example, see data on Chicago and Washington cited in "Integration Battlefront," *Journal of the National Medical Association*, 55 (1963), 349–53.

[32] Henrik L. Blum and Alvin R. Leonard, *Public Administration—A Public Health Viewpoint*. (New York: Macmillan, 1963), p. 21.

[33] At least a few aware administrators have questioned such pamphlets in a very basic sense, suggesting that "instead of working directly . . . to modify the attitudes of Negroes, it may be more fruitful . . . to focus on

Finally, for the few black doctors who want to at least practice medicine, even if they have little political voice, their problems are also magnified by the simple fact that it is economically difficult to establish their practices in poor black ghetto communities. A recent booklet put out by the AMA gives the following advice to doctors planning their practice: "Ideally, a physician strives to seek the proper balance between the scientific and business aspects of medicine." [34] Stressing "good management principles" and a "successful practice at minimum costs," it reflects the criteria which lead doctors to establish their practices outside ghetto areas, outside the areas of greatest need but where there is also the least ability to pay, lowest quality physical plants, and the greatest number of cost and efficiency problems. Without encouragement and special aid, establishment of a ghetto practice is a difficult operation. Thus, from medical school to medical practice, Negroes are in one way or another excluded from full participation in the medical profession.

A second major institution which contributes to the racially un-equal consequences of the American health-care system is the hospital with its associated personnel and practices. Again, the most striking feature here is that though there is a good deal of work being done now on the sociology of the hospital, there is very little data available on the racial features of current practices. Perhaps the best documented of the racial aspects of American hospitals is the segregation of hospital beds in many areas of the country. This was common practice historically, but the federally enacted Hill-Burton Hospital Survey and Construction Act of 1946 was the only piece of legislation since Reconstruction which specifically allowed for "separate but equal" health facilities. Its section 622(f) permitted federal financial support for construction of separate facilities for different population groups as long as there was equitable provision on the basis of need for facilities and services of like quality for

---

the behavior of professional personnel and organization which may constitute the most important impediments to the provision of health care to Negroes." Sol Levine, "Health Attitudes of the Negro," *Centennial Conference on the Health Status of the Negro Today and in the Future,* Howard University College of Medicine, March, 1967.

[34] *The Business Side of Medical Practice.* AMA publication, American Medical Assn., 1962.

each such group.[35] Under this law, federal funds amounting to about $1.9 billion supported some 7,750 hospitals and clinics. At least ninety-eight of these accepted no blacks, while many of the rest segregated blacks into separate wings and wards, basements and halls, and other places traditionally reserved for black patients.[36] Fourteen states thus developed whole hospital systems based on the separate but equal provision. Thus, hospital segregation was official in many areas, in addition to being *de facto* in other areas (especially the North) for the economic reasons discussed earlier. In March, 1964, ten years after "separate but equal" was stricken from education, that "separate but equal" provision of the Hill-Burton legislation was also declared unconstitutional. And then on July 2, 1964, the Civil Rights Act of 1964 became law, Title VI of which forbade racial discrimination in all federally supported programs, thus affecting nearly 5,000 institutions supported by the U.S. Public Health Service.[37]

The unfortunate truth is that the effect of this major policy change is not really known. Statistics on the racial composition of daily hospital census are not available. But what little is known indicates that compliance has been minimal in many areas. The federal office charged with enforcing the law has made most of its inquiries by mail; when actual on-site visits have been made, startling observations have been reported. On-site observers ran into "what became known as the 'HEW shuffle' where white and black patients were moved into new beds in new rooms and wards for the brief moment of the study team's visit." [38] Though HEW is optimistic, 215 hospitals decided not to accept federal funds and thereby remain beyond the reach of Title VI. But even when hospitals comply, subtle discrimination is

easy to carry on today because modern hospital design discourages large wards. Usually rooms accommodate two to six patients. Hos-

[25] Cited in "Integration Battlefront," *Journal of the National Medical Association*, 55 (1963), 339.
[26] *Ibid.*, p. 342.
[27] Luther Terry, "Hospitals and Title VI of the Civil Rights Act," *Hospitals*, 39 (1965), 34–37.
[38] Robert Nash, "Compliance of Hospitals and Health Agencies with Title VI of the Civil Rights Act," *American Journal of Public Health*, 58 (1968), 246–51.

pital admitting clerks assign "compatible" patients to the same room. "Compatibility" frequently means that all patients in a room are either white or Negro. Although the "compatibility" criterion is used out of a solicitude for the supposed feelings of the white patient, the feelings of the ailing Negro are ignored and his health jeopardized.[39]

Thus, the combination of historical tradition, lack of federal willingness to aggressively document compliance to federal law, and local willingness to operate hospitals which were either intentionally segregated or in fact separated due to their geographical location or the means of payment for services has resulted in poorly documented but apparently considerable racial segregation of hospital services. (It may seem unfair, but the time has come to assume discrimination until proven otherwise.) At some of these levels, the racist attitudes of the individuals in power are no doubt a major factor; but the overwhelming structural and institutional factor is the lack of black participation in the decision-making apparatus. Although detailed statistics are not available, there seems little reason to doubt the subjective impression that blacks are, on a national basis, very poorly represented on the hospital boards and staffs which establish local hospital policy regarding admission and hospital location. And even in the white community, patients who are poor have essentially no voice in the decision-making process. Thus, the essence of racism in hospitals seems to be white paternalism—upper-class whites on the whole control the economic resources needed to build hospitals, and they control the bodies which govern those hospitals. So, whether the hospitals are desegregated or not and at what rate is all at the pleasure of the whites who control the system. This structural exclusion of the blacks from power seems to be the basis of the racially imbalanced admission practices.

A second way in which American hospitals contribute to racially unequal consequences is through their employment and promotion practices. Casual observation verifies that the lower the position in the hospital employment-authority hierarchy, the more likely it is that the position will be filled by a nonwhite minority-group person.

---

[39] *Health Care and the Negro Population,* p. 11.

Blacks are very underrepresented at the nurse-administrator level and very overrepresented at the orderly-janitorial level. The actual employment statistics for this situation (as usual) are not available, but it is well reflected in nursing school data. In 1965–66, blacks accounted for only 3.2 per cent of all admissions to schools of nursing. In the same year, blacks were 18.8 per cent of the admissions to schools granting the professionally less advanced Associate degree in practical nursing. Of all the students graduating that same year, blacks were 3.4 per cent of all RN's and 16.3 per cent of all practical nurses.[40] This, of course, reflects to some degree the candidates' previous education and is therefore partially a product of the racial inequalities in college education. But the hospitals support this racial separation by tolerating an artificial separation of professional strata within their employment system. It is not possible for an extremely competent practical nurse to profit by her experience and in-service training, in the form of promotion across rigid professional strata, to assume the duties of an RN which she may be fully competent to carry out. Clearly, this is not solely the fault of the hospital, but the hospital condones it, and in this way the institutional structure of the hospital supports a system which has obvious analogies to the tracking system present in the educational institutions. For reasons which have nothing to do with the ability of a person to do a given job, institutional formality dictates promotional procedures which maintain a racial imbalance within the authority hierarchy. Thus, procedures developed in the name of professional excellence have the result of discriminating against black people, keeping blacks from rising to positions of control, and producing racist consequences throughout the institutions.

Consideration of the problem of racism in health institutions leads to the generalization that institutions tend to become self-perpetuating with less responsiveness to the goals they were intended to fulfill. The American health institutions are not charged with maintaining the present system of health care; rather, their social function is to promote the health of the American people by whatever mechanism is best. Insofar as they are not pursuing this

[40] National League for Nursing, "Educational Preparation for Nursing, 1966," *Nursing Outlook*, 15 (1967), 64–68.

goal, they betray their own stagnation. That health institutions have not adequately responded to the needs of black people is clear; that this is the case because black people have been kept out of the decision-making structure of the institutions is becoming clear. The needs of a people which are neither seen nor heard will probably not be met.

So far, the rate at which black people are gaining voice in the health system seems hopelessly slow. There has, however, been one recent development which offers some indication of the capacity of the health institutions for self-renewal, for adaptation to meet the health needs of all Americans. This is the neighborhood health center, which is being tested in several black communities. In many ways a new institution, several features common to nearly all of these centers are of special interest. First, these centers are headed by a board of directors composed of representative members of the community served, thus insuring greater responsiveness to the community's desires and needs. Second, the centers are located in the community itself and operate during hours which are convenient for that community. Third, the emphasis in patient care is not on medical treatment alone but on taking action to best promote the total health of the patient, this being facilitated by the use of inter-disciplinary health teams rather than just a medically oriented physician alone. Fourth, community people are recruited to work in the center. Local people are paid to increase communication between the community and the center itself, bridging the information gap by whatever means are appropriate. Professional stratification is eliminated wherever possible—plans call for promotion according to competence rather than by college courses completed. Finally, many of the centers see their role not as just a dispenser of medical care but also as an advocate of "extra-medical" social change where this is necessary to promote the total health of the individual or the community as a whole. Such centers are no panacea, for they too are dependent on the benevolence of white-controlled government health financing; but they do serve as prototypes which may suggest other ways of eliminating racism in this country's health institutions, ways which will produce meaningful change at a rate determined by black people.

In conclusion, three basic statements can summarize this section on racism in health institutions:

1. The goal of all people working in the health institutions can never be simply the expansion and perpetuation of those institutions. The goal must be the best possible health for all the people by whatever means necessary.

2. Basic health statistics show that this aim has not been accomplished in this country. Health in 1968 in the United States of America is a racially distributed commodity.

3. The failure of the institutions to correct this injustice can be traced partly to the fact that the system rations health according to purchasing power rather than need. But more basically, these institutions fail because their control is vested in an essentially closed panel of white professionals who are not representative of all health professionals, let alone all patients who are to be served. This lack of representation allows bigotry in a few cases and ignorance in most cases to prevail at decision-making levels and results in actions which have racist results. Until black people have some control of the decisions which directly affect their health and health care, the white health institutions will continue to support the overall pattern of institutional racism.

Chapter 8

From No Response to False Response

From the first Supreme Court school desegregation decision in 1954 to President Johnson's War on Poverty, the federal government has compiled a record of civil rights action with an impressive appearance. The use of federal troops in Little Rock and the forcible desegregation of southern schools in several other areas convinced many Americans that the government was ready to put force behind its pronounced policies. In 1964, President Johnson committed the nation to an "unconditional War on Poverty . . . because it is right, because it is wise, and because for the first time in our history, it is possible to conquer poverty."

In the private sectors of American life, business, labor, religious organizations, and other national institutions have echoed in their statements the government's concern to eliminate segregation and discrimination. Virtually all openly racist clauses have been removed from union charters and real estate contracts. The large industries have committed themselves to equal opportunity hiring practices and in some cases to job training programs for the unemployed.

With all the legislation and policy changes of the past fourteen years the country appears to have made major progress toward solving the racial problem. But appearances are deceptive; behind the highly publicized victories for racial justice there exists a vast reservoir of ineffectiveness. The dismal history of the riots of the 1960's and the subsequent findings of the Kerner Commission testify em-

115

phatically to the failure of most of that which has gone before. The poor are still very poor, the slums remain crowded, and the War on Poverty has been reduced to a minor skirmish.

It is clear now that the nation has not responded in any significant manner to liberal leadership. Many individuals and institutions, including government agencies, have chosen to avoid compliance with the new laws in a display of callous illegality. Those that do attempt a positive response to the crisis are too often satisfied with token gestures that may salve the conscience but do not contribute to a national solution. Frequently welfare and poverty programs have fallen into a damaging paternalism, or they have been so dominated by the concept of assimilation that they have lost all touch with the realities of the chasm between the races. In addition to all these problems of motivation, countless programs go on the rocks simply because of poor judgment which grows out of misinformation and inexperience in the field of social action. Social reform at the present time is not a profession, not a science, but a hodge-podge of amateurs spurred on by a number of different ideologies and rationales that are only tenuously related to each other. There is little wonder that many failures are the result of sheer incompetence.

NONCOMPLIANCE

By the device of equal laws, unequally applied, Negro Americans are being denied the right and opportunity to vote and discrimination is given sanction under color of law. Varieties of techniques (to avoid compliance) are infinite. Three are most commonplace. 1. The technique of technical "error" . . . 2. The technique of noncooperation . . . 3. The technique of subjective tests . . . Whatever the technique, the intended purpose of such devices is effectively served.

LYNDON BAINES JOHNSON

The impact of the series of civil rights laws has been greatly reduced from what it could have been because many of the individuals and institutions affected by the laws have refused to comply. There is sufficient evidence to demonstrate that this reluctance to change on the part of local centers of power is aided and abetted by a corresponding reluctance within the federal government to enforce its own laws. National attention is drawn to the passage of a bill, and the liberal politicians are thereby assured of retaining the minority vote. But the extended process of enforcement or non-enforcement is rarely reviewed by the mass media and is therefore usually unknown to the public.

Examples of "paper decrees" are numerous in every area associated with human and civil rights—in justice, welfare, law enforcement, and employment, to name a few. A good example of non-compliance can be found in the campaign for integrated schools, the issue that first brought civil rights to national attention.

In 1954, the Supreme Court ruled that separate facilities were "inherently unequal" and that segregated schools would no longer be legal. Another generation of children passed through the schools before Congress finally admitted that nothing was being done and passed the 1964 Civil Rights Act. According to the 1964 Act, a school district that did not desegregate was subject to the penalty of loss of all federal funds.

The impotence of the 1964 Act has been well documented. Take, for instance, the schools of a moderate border state, Virginia. In the 1965–66 school year, 124 of the 130 school districts in the state of Virginia were listed as being "in compliance." However, of the 239,000 black children in those "desegregated" districts, only 26,300 were enrolled in schools with whites. Most of the districts fell far short of federal projections of percentages of students in integrated schools for 1966. Yet the federal enforcement program was *cut back* in Virginia rather than strengthened. Meanwhile, federal funds continued to flow into most districts.

The Virginia school situation is not an isolated incident of federal laxity. Congress has cut the total amount of funds originally allocated for enforcement of all the antisegregation clauses of the 1964 Act. The U.S. Commission on Civil Rights in 1965 reported that in the South:

1. There continues to be widespread segregation or exclusion of Negroes in federally assisted programs at the state and local level.

2. The Department of Health, Education, and Welfare, after drafting and issuing the regulations and formal documents required thereunder, has failed to take the steps necessary to achieve compliance.

3. The failure to adopt adequate review and compliance procedures has made it impossible for the Department of HEW to know whether discrimination is actually being eliminated.

4. The Department of HEW has not provided state and local directors and administrators of federally assisted programs with the information, support, and leadership necessary to facilitate compliance under Title 6 of the Civil Rights Act of 1964.[1]

Noncompliance with desegregation policies does not occur in government structures alone. In 1955 when the AFL–CIO was formed, it pledged to "encourage all workers, regardless of race, creed, or color, to share equally in the benefits of union organization." Yet a 1960 census showed that there were only 2,191 black apprentices in all trades throughout the country, *one more than in 1950*. The Brotherhood of Railway and Steamship Clerks did away with its "white" and "colored" job classifications by hiring whites for jobs traditionally reserved for black men, who were then left jobless. Furthermore, unions continue to use their legal resources to *defend* locals in court suits involving discrimination, rather than seeking to eliminate racist practices.

Examples can be drawn from all parts of the nation and all types of organizations to demonstrate the extent of noncompliance in lower echelons and the great lack of enforcement from the top. The public must be aware that the passage of a civil rights law which is not obeyed or enforced can only lead to greater injustice and increased frustration and tension. Disrespect for the law starts in white society, and until white society stops its "open defiance of the law," as it is called by the President's Commission on Civil Disorders, there can be no hope of even beginning to fight racism and injustice.

[1] U.S. Commission on Civil Rights, *Title 6—One Year After* (Washington, D.C.: Government Printing Office), pp. 45–46.

TOKENISM

People rarely want to face the full magnitude of a social problem. Most Americans operate on the unarticulated theory that if everyone gave just a little more to Community Chest and if all businesses hired one black man, the American crisis would be solved. While the ranks of the unemployed grow and life in the slums deteriorates still further, the average liberal American feels that he has done his part if he has asked his Congressman to support open housing or donated to the local relief fund. People resist having their eyes opened to the fact that isolated acts of charity are totally incommensurate with the size of the task before the nation.

Tokenism is operative on the scale of government as well as in the case of the individual. The miniscule percentage of the national budget that goes to the War on Poverty is in fact a token effort in the face of the awesome magnitude of the problem in the cities. Priorities tell the story. Between 1960 and 1967, we have spent $348 billion on war, $27 billion on space, and $2 billion on community development and housing.[2]

Tokenism is found within government programs designed specifically to alleviate the effects of poverty and discrimination. Upward Bound is a federally funded project designed to combat the educational deficiencies that result from ghetto school conditions. Funds are supplied to a college for a six- to eight-week summer program in which a group of several dozen ghetto children who are deemed to be of college potential are given intensive training to raise their chances of entering higher education. There are numerous flaws in the structure of the program, such as that community participation is negligible. But the most damaging criticism is that while school districts continue to miseducate thousands upon thousands of black children, the talents of numerous skilled educators and organizers are tied up in an attempt to save forty or fifty exceptional students. Upward Bound is a token effort because it strikes not at the root of the problem but only at a symptom of the basic ill.

[2] W. H. Ferry, "Farewell to Integration," *The Center Magazine*, I (March 1968), 36.

PATERNALISM

Social scientists, social planners, and prosperous white people in general often exhibit a racist condescension toward the ghetto residents about whom they are so concerned. Rather than treating the poor as adults who know well what they lack and what they want, whites too often act as though black people were irresponsible children who cannot be trusted with power even in their own communities. Black people understandably find the paternalistic attitude particularly obnoxious. They sense a lack of candor and self-critical honesty among people who will donate old clothes or Christmas baskets but who never even speak to the slumlord who may be their next-door neighbor in the suburb. Programs that rest on a paternalistic assumption contain the seeds of their own demise. The black man will either reject them as an offense to his humanity, or he will be forced to lose his self-respect to cooperate.

A naive, stupid paternalism is exhibited by most church benevolences, by the white person who gives groceries to a welfare family and then retreats to suburban security, or by the white teacher who seeks to instill "responsibility" and the work-ethic in ghetto youth who cannot get a job no matter how clean and tidy they are. A more calculated, destructive form of paternalism is rampant within the welfare and OEO bureaucracies.

The welfare program in most cities is based on the assumption that the recipient is a shiftless, ne'er-do-well who cannot be trusted with more than a subsistence income.

> Applicants are invariably subject to elaborate, lengthy, demeaning initial investigations, apparently based on the presumption that they are chiselers until proven otherwise. Once receiving assistance they are constantly harassed by unannounced visits to their homes, by searches and seizures, and by countless other outrageous invasions of their privacy. . . . Welfare authorities are so involved in the highly expensive process of investigation that little time is left for providing basic services. New York's Commissioner of Welfare,

Mitchell I. Ginsberg, acknowledges that his welfare staff spends 70 per cent of its time checking on and investigating applicants.[3]

The War on Poverty produced one program that was initially aimed at overcoming the barrier of federal paternalism. This was the Community Action Program. (See Chapter 6.) President Johnson declared to Congress, "Through a new community action program we intend to strike at poverty at its source. . . . This asks men and women throughout the country to prepare long-range plans for the attack on poverty in their own local communities. These are not plans prepared in Washington and imposed upon hundreds of different situations. They are based on the fact that local citizens best understand their own problems, and best know how to deal with these problems." Most important, the act declared that a "community action program means a program which . . . is developed, conducted, and administered with the maximum feasible participation of the groups served . . ."[4]

The concept of giving the poor money and power to shape their own programs and lives was a bold one—and a threatening one to the city hall, welfare, and other establishment bureaucrats across the country. OEO was threatening to create a new basis for political power, one which brought into being new leaders and new organizations, which would control money and jobs, and which would not be beholden to city hall or other government agencies.

After the act was passed and communities began organizing antipoverty councils and drawing up plans for CAP programs, groups made up, by and large, of social work professionals, public officials, and civic and business leaders sought to shape and control the programs. Sometimes "representatives" of the poor were allowed in—but even they were usually selected by some welfare official or a representative of the mayor's office.

In Chicago, for example, twelve out of the sixty-member council are ostensibly representatives from six poverty areas, but they are

[3] See, for instance, U.S. Senate, Committee on Labor and Public Welfare, Staff and Consultants Report, *Examination of the War on Poverty* (Washington, D.C.: Government Printing Office, September 1967).
[4] "Lyndon Johnson's Poverty Message to Congress," *The War on Poverty, Economic Opportunity Act of 1964*, March 16, 1964.

selected by the politically appointed administrators of the "service centers" in the six areas. In New York, the city government ". . . finally agreed that the council against poverty would be one-third poor. However, the city declared it illegal for the council to receive funds, so an office called the Economic Opportunity Committee, with no poor representation, was set up as the program's fiscal agent." [5]

Sargent Shriver, the director of the War on Poverty, was severely criticized by Congressman Adam Clayton Powell at the House hearing on the CAP program. Charged Powell, "In Cleveland, the mayor appointed the first board there, as you know, of twenty-two people, and he appointed fifteen people from outside of Cleveland, who lived in the suburbs . . . ! The people who have kept the poor impoverished were appointed, from Shaker Heights, and from wealthy suburbia of Cleveland and to direct the War on Poverty program. As you know, and as I have repeated and repeated, this must be changed." [6]

The paternalistic approach to poverty and the racial ghetto remains the predominant mode of response from charitable individuals and government officials. Paternalism is a failure to respond in that it further ingrains in society the impotent status of the poor and the black. Rather than opening the doors of escape from the ghetto, it grinds black people under the heel of a myopic bureaucracy.

ASSIMILATION

Countless programs fail to make inroads into the racist status quo because they implicitly assume that black people must become "white" in order to enter the mainstream of society. White administrators often seem more concerned about changing the attitudes and mores of black people than they do about offering them concrete opportunities to further their education or to obtain good jobs. Of

[5] David Stoloff, "The Short Unhappy History of Community Action Programs," in *The Great Society Reader*, eds. Gettleman and Mermelstein (New York: Vintage Books, 1967), pp. 235–36.

[6] Sargent Shriver, "The War on Poverty Is a Movement of Conscience," in *The Great Society Reader*, p. 212.

course, it is always easier to blame black people and their culture for the plight of the ghetto than it is to point the accusing finger at recalcitrant white employers and businessmen.

The TIDE program in Oakland was designed to help youths find jobs. The students were selected by poverty-program workers in the Bay Area; they were sixteen to twenty-two years old, mostly Negro, and received five dollars a day to participate. TIDE trained them in how to apply for jobs—how to make a good impression in an interview, how to speak well, dress properly, etc. TIDE was to act as an employment agency for white private enterprise. The program was not a success. Said one teacher, "I guess these kids just don't want jobs. The clothes they wear are loud. They don't talk decent English. They're boisterous. And they constantly fool around. They refuse to take the program seriously." [7]

Actually, the students took real job openings very seriously and studied for the required test when openings occurred. "Their desire for work was not the problem," writes the sociologist who studied the program.

> The real problem was what the program demanded of the young men. It asked that they change their manner of speech and dress, that they ignore their lack of skills and society's lack of jobs, and that they act as if their arrest records were of no consequence in obtaining a job. It asked that they pretend that they, not society, bore the responsibility for their being unemployed. TIDE didn't ask much of the men; only that they become white. [8]

Thus understood, it comes as no surprise that the TIDE workers and teachers viewed the program as an exercise in futility and concluded that the young men just "didn't want jobs."

A similar situation has developed in the nationwide Job Corps. This program was begun in 1964 as a means of making employable the "hard-core" unemployed, that is, youths who have left school and who have virtually no occupational skills.

President Johnson demanded "success" in this war. Written into the program, therefore, were several mechanisms to increase the

---

[7] David Wellman, "Putting on the Poverty Program" (Ann Arbor: Radical Education Project, no date), p. 1.

[8] David Wellman, "The Wrong Way to Find Jobs for Negroes," *Transaction*, April 1968, p. 10.

chances of success. Applicants with serious police records or with physical disabilities are denied admission. Furthermore, Job Corps administrators and screeners see seven youths for every one who is placed in the Corps. Since each administrator no doubt wishes to make his camp a model one, "problem cases" are rejected. And since the most severe "attitudinal problems" are doubtless to be found among blacks, it comes as no surprise that in the first year of operation the majority of enrollees were white. This is not to say that white youth do not need and deserve help. It simply points out that the program is not reaching the "hard-core" unemployed black teenager as it purports to do.

The type of training enrollees receive is another indication of the inadequacy and racism built into the Job Corps. The enrollment in 1967 was 42,032. Approximately half of these young men were sent to the ninety Conservation Centers. (There are only ten urban centers.) Activity at the Conservation Centers consists mostly of menial labor to improve National Forests and other recreation spots (for middle-class vacationers). Training in skills useful for urban employment is virtually nonexistent. Significantly, OEO reports that one-third of the graduates of work-training programs fail to find any work whatsoever. And of the two-thirds who do find jobs, most must settle for low-paying, unskilled labor. The Job Corps provides in its motivation training only one component of the process of social change. Because it has often failed to take seriously the need for specific skills and job openings, the Job Corps is an inauthentic response to the problem of unemployment.

The Job Corps and other similar projects fail because they rest on the assumption that cultural assimilation is the key to the solution of the racial crisis. The assimilationist attitude is, in effect, a false response because it obscures the primary need for the creation of real opportunity in employment, education, and government.

FALSE RESPONSE AND SOCIAL ILLUSIONS

There are two illusions underlying the forms of false response discussed in the preceding pages. The first illusion is that the condition of the black population is steadily improving and that it will continue to improve without drastic changes in our approach to the problem. The second myth is that poverty and racism are best fought *within* the black community.

Sufficient statistical information has been cited in the course of this book to disprove the idea that conditions within the black community are steadily improving. Certainly, relative to white economic progress, the black population has been going backwards. Without regard to the facts, the mythmakers have stifled any sense of urgency in the search for new approaches.

The second false assumption, that the poverty of the ghettos is best attacked directly through the War on Poverty, welfare, and the countless other ghetto-oriented programs, has caused white people to overlook the more basic issue of racist attitudes and institutions that shut black people off from the instruments of self-determination. A problem cannot be solved unless it is attacked at its roots, but when the roots are found entwined in the lives, communities, and occupations of white people, it is far easier for them to place the blame elsewhere than to face up to their own responsibility. The result has been an overemphasis on poverty. Since the black man's hell is created by both poverty and racism, given the choice, white policy-makers prefer to see black resentment and protest as being due to poverty. Vast welfare bureaucracies and anti-poverty programs are created to buy off and placate the rage of the black community. In the meantime, the white hegemony and wealth remain intact.

Unless this misdirection is understood and corrected, white liberals will continue to waste their energies on blunders in the black community without appreciably altering racial inequities.

Epilogue

The Way Out: Looking at White Society

Our analysis of institutional racism has led us to an examination of the manner in which practices disadvantageous to blacks but advantageous to whites operate through the structures and institutions of American society. We have seen that white-controlled institutions have failed to provide black citizens with the means for a relevant and meaningful education, a voice in political processes, the rights of economic self-determination, just treatment under the law, or decent health care. Our intent has not been to provide an exhaustive description of all the ways in which institutional racism operates in the society, and many readers will have by now added their own examples. Rather our intent has been to provide, for ourselves as well as our readers, a way of looking at racism which might suggest more effective methods for eliminating this outrage in American society.

The initial chapter posited that racism was a "white problem" and as such must be solved in the white community. Racism will not be ended by the normal working of institutions whose very normality is itself the foundation of the racial problem. If racism is sustained by the status quo, and if the status quo is in turn sustained by a "business as usual" mentality, then only something *unusual* will reverse the direction our nation is bent upon. Something "unusual," we believe, must take place in the institutions of white America.

It is not easy to suggest unusual remedies. Our conventional wisdom tends to severely restrict the range of alternatives considered when social reform is under discussion. But, if our analysis is correct, American society needs to expand greatly its understanding of "the possible"—what is seen as possible must come to include major revisions in institutional arrangements. One manner in which our understanding might be expanded is to pose a question thus far ignored in our analysis. As we have seen, racism is a white problem in the sense that it involves the manner in which white institutions penalize citizens with black skins. But, might not racism be a white problem in another sense as well, in the sense that it adversely affects white people as well as blacks? Chapter 4, "The Miseducation of White Children" points to a "yes" answer to this question. There we saw that the falsification of American history and the ethnocentrism rampant within white schools cannot help but misshape the education of white children. There can be no psychology of black inferiority without a psychology of white supremacy. In this sense, the children in white schools are victims. They see themselves and others through eyeglasses which distort and misrepresent. Many whites live with a fear of black people, a fear which in an extreme case can blossom into acute paranoia and hysteria. And under conditions of social tension the number of "extreme cases" can become all too many. It is not rare today to hear whites make the incredible assertion that the "niggers are taking over." At the very least, then, the racism in white society is as psychologically damaging to whites as it is to blacks.

Are there other ways in which racism might affect the white community? We can partially answer this question through an autobiographical excursion that shows something about what happened to a group of white students as they attempted to address themselves to the "race question." As outlined in the Preface, our group came together in the fall of 1967 to study racism and its effects on a black community and to examine how we, as whites, could work to eliminate the effects of racial prejudice. Our motives for entering the work-study project varied greatly from individual to individual. And though we verbalized a rejection of "white paternalism"— going to the black community to help poor blacks—most of us probably felt we were working on behalf of the black movement.

In addition to doing the research for this book, we attended numerous meetings in the white community, meetings at which the decisions affecting the lives of black citizens were being made. We also initiated and participated in seminars at Stanford University and in the local white community which attempted to explain "black power" to white audiences. Since most self-respecting blacks had given up trying to pry open white eyes, we found ourselves in frequent demand. We soon were seen by white liberals as "nigger experts," as people who presumably knew what was happening in the black community and could interpret it to white student groups, churches, civic associations, and so forth. Thus, although initially justifying our activity in terms of blacks and their oppressed condition, we became most active in the white community.

As the year progressed, we became more and more involved in talking to white groups and in trying to change white institutions. This experience was not an easy one. The earlier definitions of ourselves and our group began to change, a change which was subtle and confusing to most of us. We began to lose the clear sense we had of ourselves as white supporters of the black struggle for freedom. We became increasingly frustrated by our inability to move white institutions in any new and creative directions. Some of us began to think more carefully about our own future, about the military draft, the limited career opportunities available to those committed to social change, and the dismaying prospect of life in white, middle-class suburbia. We began, in effect, to sense our own alienation from the centers of decision-making and power. This revelation of our own powerlessness came as something of a shock. As children of the white, affluent culture, we had been taught that we were able to participate in the determination of our destinies. We were entitled to the vote when we were of age. We could write letters to our representatives and complain to the city council if something really disturbed our tranquillity. And, in truth, government and institutions *did* work for us as long as we were content to stay within the boundaries of acceptable opinion. But to actually suggest that white institutions—the university we attended, the churches we belonged to, the political arrangements of the community in which we were tax-paying citizens, the local board of the schools where we might someday send our children, the police force presumably hired to enforce fair laws, the hospitals whose services were available to us—begin to change in ways which would eliminate racism was to step outside those boundaries.

And we suspect that in increasing numbers other white Americans are learning that they must raise "unusual" questions and search for "unusual" political forms. First, the hard revelation of poverty, hunger, and black oppression, then the growing awareness of the pollution of the environment, and more recently the fear of a military-industrial complex not under the control of the American electorate has precipitated a crisis of conscience and of confidence in parts of white America. Liberals are discovering that these vast problems are not soluble through standard political process—through voting Democratic, through letters to Congress, through testimony at city council. The national institutional structure is not responding in any adequate way to the life and death issues that plague the nation. Even whites are beginning to feel the frustration and fears of powerlessness in the face of those institutions that once seemed so protective.

A system of compromise has long been operative between institutional leaders and the people of the white community. Whites were allowed to ignore the deterioration of the inner city as long as they were willing to move progressively farther into the monotonous suburbs; they could overlook smog and traffic death tolls if they were content with the comforts and freedom of a Detroit sedan; they could forget about the tax dollars spent on death in Vietnam as long as the violence was "over there." But the wages of negligence are coming due very rapidly: guerilla war in our cities becomes increasingly probable; the pollution of the environment has reached an unforeseen level; suburbs threaten to swallow up open space; more Americans have been killed in Vietnam than in Korea. The old compromises have broken down. A new course must be plotted, new power arrangements must be created before the nation unravels. We believe solutions will be found only as the people band together to demand a reordering of priorities and a new system of popular participation in decision-making. We conclude our analysis with some suggestions for first steps toward organized action against racism in the white community.

WHAT CAN WE DO?

The various institutional areas covered in the preceding chapters should provide many ideas about specific issues upon which an anti-racist organization can concentrate its energies. Whether or not there is a black community near at hand, there are many matters that deserve the attention of action groups in the white community. For example, are schools preparing their students to appreciate the cultures of other racial and ethnic groups, and are children exposed to the historical truth about white racism? Is adequate housing available in the community for people of all different income levels, including welfare recipients? Are local schools, churches, and government careful to buy goods and services only from businesses that are actively seeking to hire more black and minority employees at all levels of the pay scale? These are questions that are applicable in any white community, be it a metropolis or a village. Our analysis and all the information that has come to light in the past decade indicates that the answers to such questions will be universally negative. A campaign organized around multicultural education, low-income housing, or selective buying could be the beginning of an antiracism movement in communities that have not yet begun to think of racism as their own problem.

In areas that lie closer to black communities, antiracist organizations should directly support black demands for self-determination. White activists in such situations have a responsibility to interpret to their own community how black demands relate to the welfare of all citizens. It is also important to demonstrate how the institutions that oppress black people, such as police forces, slumlords, and centralized, insensitive school boards, are firmly rooted in the white community. White support of such oppressive arrangements should be challenged by means such as campaigns for civilian review boards, strict enforcement of building codes, and local participation in control of schools.

Although the task appears overwhelming, if one institution can be forced to examine its policies and their implications for the exclusion of black people, then a chain-reaction of ferment may develop in other areas. The overall picture of racism must not discourage groups from selecting a single issue that lies near at hand. A concerted drive to establish low-income housing in a white suburb, for example, will in itself reveal much about zoning ordinances, private financers, real-estate interests, banks, city councils, and planning commissions. Even though public housing may not be realized, this campaign itself, if properly conducted and publicized, would shake people out of their false sense of noninvolvement and plant the seeds of change which could grow to fruition in some unforeseen way.

HOW CAN IT BE ACCOMPLISHED?

An individual working alone can do very little about racism in American institutional life; he will be swallowed up by the sheer size of the problem. To work for institutional change it is necessary to develop a force for change in the community, and no one person can constitute that force. Therefore, a first suggestion would be that the individual get together with friends, fellow workers, and neighbors in the area who share similar concerns. Initially, the group must develop a rough analysis of the ways local institutions operate and how they contribute to the subordination and exploitation of black people.

Second, the organization must get down to specific issues as soon as possible. Most American people are tired of sweeping generalities and vague statements. If they are seriously ready to work on racism, then they should be able to dig right into a particular issue that has a bearing on their own lives. It is often useful to divide the beginning group into task forces on specific subjects (i.e., housing, welfare, media, employment, education). Each subgroup should have a center of one or two people who will accept responsibility to recruit other workers.

Third, the task forces should find out who else is already working in the areas of concern and consult them immediately. Very often much time and research effort can be saved by learning from others who have been working on the issue for a longer time. Duplication of effort should be avoided.

Workers should beware of false distinctions between education and action. There are many ways to learn—reading and study being only one of them. A little study on a particular issue should lead to some concrete proposals and suggestions about how to act. For example, one such group, after studying their local housing authority, found that the authority had not done anything in twenty-seven years to promote housing for poor and minority people. The task force and its supporters then began attending meetings of that authority with proposals for what it should have been doing. As they became more involved with trying to move the authority, they learned more about the way the commission functioned, to whom it was responsive, and where it could be moved in the future. The same dynamic holds true for most institutions. The more people become involved in attempting to change the institution, the more they learn about institutional change—where it is possible and where it is not. An organization should not get bogged down in "armchair" strategizing. Members will learn faster about the dynamics of change by practice and experience.

Both patience and a firm commitment must be maintained for a successful campaign. Racism is complex and deeply imbedded within the fabric of our present structures, and it will not be rooted out in three months or three years. On the other hand, the problem is clearly a pressing one, and a start should be made immediately. The trick is to maintain a commitment throughout all the frustrations and disappointments that an organization is likely to encounter in attempting to change the way in which an institution functions.

Finally, any group has to have confidence in itself in order to draw more people into its campaign. It does not take a professionally paid "organizer" to get people moving. Anyone who is reasonably personable, has confidence in his organization and its goals, and is able to meet and talk to new people can be a good organizer. To involve others in attempts to change situations, members must be ready to go to interested people, talk to them, explain why they feel their campaign is important, and encourage them to become involved. A group may wish to form speaking teams of one long-standing, experienced member and one newer worker.

Organizing need not be a painful experience. People should work in a situation where they feel at home. Union members should work with other union members; professionals may organize within their associations. Churchmen may find an effective avenue through a social action committee. A local action group in California was initiated by a small group of dedicated women who used coffees as their major organizing means. Imagination is always an important resource. Every day presents countless opportunities to involve oneself and others in movements to effect social change.

Perhaps the real question is one of commitment, whether or not white people really want to do something. It appears that many people who seem to be asking "What can I do?" actually are asking "What can I do without changing anything?" If there is no commitment to changing the institutions of white society, the concerned white citizen can do little about racism. In order to combat racism effectively in our present society, we must overcome our fears of change and be willing to work actively to reorder our society.

For too long American society has believed in the mythology that social ills are in truth nothing but the aggregate of individual defects. If a black man is unemployed or uneducated or poorly housed, it must be due to some failure to "achieve" on his part. Or, if we do not directly place blame on his character defects, we suggest that there is some prejudiced employer or inadequate teacher or bigoted realtor who is bringing about the condition. As our analysis attempts to make clear, and as the chapter by Harold Baron which follows illustrates in rich detail, some social ills are not adequately explained by simply alluding to individual defects. There are social ills which are structured into the very operations of the society, which are inevitable given the institutional arrangements. It is this premise which bids us urge the concerned white to think in terms of organization and new institutions if he would do something about racism. We remind the reader of our dedication phrase: "institutions made by men can be changed by men."

Appendix

The Web of Urban Racism

Harold M. Baron

*It is conceivable that the Negro question—given the moral flab-
biness of America—is incapable of solution. Perhaps not all social
problems are soluble. Indeed it is only in America that one finds the
imperative to assume that all social problems can be solved without
conflict. To feel that a social problem cannot be solved peacefully is
considered immoral. Americans are required to appear cheerful and
optimistic about a solution, regardless of evidence to the contrary.
This is particularly difficult for Negroes, who at the same time must
endure all the disadvantages of the Job Ceiling and the Black
Ghetto, as well as other forms of subordination.*

*So far, most Chicagoans view Negro-white relations negatively—
solely in terms of preventing a riot.* While all responsible Negroes
try to prevent violent conflict, their primary interest is the complete
abolition of political and economic subordination and enforced
segregation.[1]

Racism has been a major, but greatly neglected, theme in the history and culture of the United States. Whatever expression the
justification and explanations of racism have taken, they have consistently rationalized underlying social relationships of domination
and exploitation of persons of African ancestry. The institutional
forms for this control of black people have undergone large-scale

[1] St. Clair Drake and Horace Cayton, *Black Metropolis: A Study of
Negro Life in a Northern City* (New York: Harcourt, Brace and Co.,
1945), p. 776. A revised and enlarged two volume edition appeared in
1962 (New York and Evanston: Harper & Row, Inc.).

134

transformations: from slavery to peonage and Jim Crow, to the web of urban racism. For the present era, it is within the institutional life of metropolitan America—North, West, and South—that the most characteristic structures of racial subjugation are found. Therefore, American racism today cannot be understood apart from the operation of the major social systems within the large cities.

Once there was a time when the reality of racial oppression in the major metropolitan areas was shielded from the view of many white eyes by the welter of seemingly impersonal, market-like relationships that characterize the city. Within the last few years the thrust of the oppressed black people has ripped off that veil, making it easier to discern the underlying social mechanisms and control systems that regulate relations between the races in the modern urban environment. The task at hand in this essay involves a working out of the concepts necessary for comprehending the basic processes of urban racism. Much of the illustrative material is taken from Chicago, which is perhaps the best-studied city in the world. While on the one hand this procedure makes the essay into somewhat of a case study, on the other hand, it is designed to set forth an analytical framework for understanding racism in any major American city.

Before we can comprehend the complex institutions of the present, we must first sketch some of the more important features of their past. Recent scholarship has shown that on the eve of colonizing the New World the English already had an image of the black African as a person apart—an outsider, barbarian, and un-Christian. However, not until a new society was established in North America did they establish the mechanisms for simultaneously incorporating and controlling blacks within a colonial extension of their own culture. "Negro slavery, a product of innumerable decisions of self-interest made by traders and princes in Europe and Africa," as Professor David Davis has recently pointed out, "was an intrinsic part of American development from the first discoveries. The evolution of the institution was also coeval with the creation of the idea of America as a new beginning, a land of promise where men's hopes and aspirations would find fulfillment." [2] In turn, racism was coeval with American slavery.

[2] David Brion Davis, *The Problem of Slavery in Western Culture* (Ithaca: Cornell University Press, 1966), pp. 24, 282–86.

The southern plantation system in the days of slavery was the cradle of the original social arrangements that made racism such a lusty offspring of American society. The rapid growth of the new nation was largely based on the exploitation of the black man as a chattel in its fertile fields. For the surpluses of tobacco and cotton so produced provided the export goods for the rapid accumulation of capital which made this nation a major economic power in an exceedingly short period of time. This class control of black slaves took on other dimensions of subjugation when race was added to economic position as a mark of social status. Comparative historical studies conclude that slavery in the United States "handstamped the status of slave upon the Black with a clarity which elsewhere could never have been so profound. . . ."[3] As a particular feature of the nation's history,

> . . . the Negro became identified with the slave, and the slave with the eternal pariah for whom there could be no escape. The slave could not ordinarily become a free man, and if chance and good fortune conspired to endow him with freedom, he still remained a Negro, and as a Negro, according to the prevailing belief, he carried all of the imputation of slave inside him.[4]

Southern society, erected upon inequality of men in law and economics, promulgated the doctrine *that slavery was a positive good.* Through the generalization of slavery's disabilities to Negroes as a race, the nonslaveholding whites were provided a symbolic stake in the system.

> While uniting the various economically divergent groups of whites, the concept of race also strengthened the ardor of most Southerners to fight for the preservation of slavery. All slaves belonged to a degraded, "inferior" race, and by the same token, all whites however wretched some of them might be, were superior. In a race-conscious society, whites at the lowest rung could identify themselves with the most privileged and efficient of the community.[5]

[3] Stanley Elkins, *Slavery, A Problem in American Institutional and Intellectual Life* (Chicago: University of Chicago Press, 1959), p. 61.
[4] Frank Tannenbaum, *Slave and Citizen: The Negro in the Americas* (New York: Vintage Books, 1946), pp. 106–7.
[5] John Hope Franklin, *The Militant South 1800–1861* (Boston: Beacon Press, 1956), p. 85.

By this process, racism became something over and above the slave system in which it had originated.

American slavery's racist definition of blacks was fundamentally accepted in the North, even though only small pockets of blacks resided there. This acceptance of racism provided the irony that during the first half of the nineteenth century northern states concomitantly did away with slavery and erected a system of racial proscription for all persons of color. In 1860, on the eve of the Civil War, "despite some notable advance, the northern Negro remained largely disenfranchised, segregated, and economically oppressed." [6]

Abolition of slavery did not mean the abolition of racism. Through the course of the Civil War and Reconstruction, northerners did away with the national power of the slave-owning class. In the course of this operation, they were forced to free the slaves and to rely on the political support of the freedmen. Then once the reins of national power were uncontestably in their hands, the northern bourgeoisie were willing to allow a counterrevolution in the South. The Compromise of 1877 brought "reunion and reaction." Through violence and disenfranchisement, black men were again reduced to powerlessness. The southern restoration reinforced the plantation system with many new varieties of labor control such as peonage and sharecropping. Racism took on a new institutional form in which it was still effective in subjugating blacks and politically disarming poor whites. However, with the loss of its decisive pre-Civil War national power, this new form of southern racism was less able to protect its system from erosion within and without.

CONTROL, CONFLICT, AND COMMUNITY

American racism has primarily been an affair in black and white. Although such other minorities as Indians, Orientals, and Spanish-speaking groups have been subjected to racial degradation and exploitation in this nation, the dominant institutional forms of American racism have been erected for the subjugation of persons

[6] Leon Litwack, *North of Slavery: The Negro in the Free States, 1790–1860* (Chicago: University of Chicago Press, 1961), p. 279.

of African ancestry. While it is both necessary and correct to emphasize the political and economic structures that form the framework of the racist system, certain aspects of social interaction have to be seen as filling out the structure. The control systems have been bolstered in the abstract by ideological justifications, institutionally by normative prescriptions, and individually by adjustments to roles either of superordination for white or subordination for blacks. The saliency of racism in American society is indicated by its pervasiveness in all areas of life from the most formal operations of government to the most casual types of interpersonal contact.

The historic durability of racism is amazing in the light of its most turbulent history. In none of its various institutional forms has it been a smoothly functioning system. Conflict and contradiction have characterized it from the beginning. For the nation as a whole, more constitutional crises have grown out of issues created by racism than from any other single cause. Many of the nation's sectional distinctions and conflicts were largely defined by differences in race and systems of racial controls. Such sectional differentiation provided the fundamental dividing line for the Civil War, the bloodiest conflict in American history.

Racial containment has always had its countertheme of sabotage, protest, and resistance. The slave system, for all its paternalism, required the lash to goad the resistant laborer on and the patrol to apprehend runaways and forestall potential revolts. Legal and political action, protest, and open resistance have been constant themes in Negro life since the Civil War. The massive reliance upon police power as an instrument of control over black communities in the cities is perhaps the best current evidence of this underlying conflict.

Racism's prescribed role of abasement and subordination for Negroes has been consistently contested. Rebels have cast off this role altogether. More frequently, individuals have developed additional roles or modes of action which would bestow some dignity and freedom. Surreptitious resistance, or the self-respect gained through mutual respect in an all-black environment provided the major means of gaining relief from the demands that racism places on one's behavior. Often, this conflict in roles became a basic conflict in one's individual personality—sometimes taking its toll, and sometimes creating amazing strength. In assessing the divergent roles of the tractable slave and the resistor, John Hope Franklin points out: "Any understanding of his reaction to his slave status must be approached with the realization that the Negro at times was possessed of a dual personality: he was one person at one time and quite a different person at another time." [7] Even for many whites too there has been conflict between the racist role of super-ordination, as a member of the dominant caste, and general equali-tarian values. In a smaller number of cases, equalitarian ways of acting have actually contended with the expected role of domina-tion. While American society's system of racial constraints has truly proved its great power in overcoming such obstacles, counterforces continue to develop.

Amidst the ordeals of suppression and resistance the black com-munity took shape. Adapting to the larger North Atlantic culture into which they had been transported by their white masters and hanging on to what could be saved from their various West African heritages, black men in America have constructed a unique com-munity. A less hardy people might well have perished, and certainly would not have persisted to become today the most decisive force for change within American life. The depth of black culture is perhaps best evidenced in that it grew and endured almost secretly beneath the monolithic racial control system of the plantation South. The strength of this culture carried on into the modern urban milieu where now it is developing self-conscious social forms for its full manifestation.

THE URBANIZATION OF RACE [8]

Little more than half a century ago, direct contact between the races took place in a milieu that was rural and southern. On the

[7] John Hope Franklin, *From Slavery to Freedom* (2nd ed., New York: Alfred A. Knopf, 1964), p. 204.
[8] This section is based upon United States Department of Labor, *The Negroes in the United States: Their Economic and Social Situation,* Bul-letin No. 1511 (June, 1966), pp. 63–70; United States Bureau of the Census, *Current Population Reports,* Series P-20, Nos. 151, 155, 157, 163,

eve of World War I, nine-tenths of the blacks in the United States lived in the South. Three-fourths of the black population, compared to one-half of the white population, lived in rural areas. Blacks composed 30 per cent of the total southern population. The life of the South and of black Americans was dominated by the plantation system and its variations of tenancy and sharecropping. Cotton was king. Even in the towns the ethos and style of the planters' world set the cultural tone.

An astounding demographic revolution has taken place in the course of fifty years. Blacks who had been a rural southern group became urban and national. By 1960, the black population was 73 per cent urban, more urban than the white population. In the North, the black population was 95 per cent urban compared to a white population that was 74 per cent urban. In the South, the urban percentages for the two groups stood respectively at 58 and 59.

The concentration of blacks in the central cities of the metropolitan areas is one of the most unique features of urban racism. As of 1966, 56 per cent of all Negroes lived in the central cities of Standard Metropolitan Statistical Areas (SMSA's). Only 27 per cent of all whites lived in central cities. Within the metropolitan areas, the growth of the black population is virtually limited to the core cities, while the growth of the white population takes place in the suburbs. In 1920, two-thirds of the metropolitan population of both races lived within the central cities and one-third in the suburban ring. From that time to 1960, 85 per cent of the increase in the metropolitan black population occurred in the central cities.

The massive shift of blacks from the southern countryside to the nation's metropolises was caused by some of the most profound economic and social developments in twentieth-century American history. Overall, it was a kind of push-pull phenomenon. The push was the displacement of blacks from southern agriculture, occasioned first by soil exhaustion, then by boll weevil destruction and

168 and Series P-25, No. 359; and Philip Hauser, "Demographic Factors in the Integration of the Negro in America," *The Negro American,* in *Daedalus: Journal of the American Academy of Arts and Sciences,* Fall, 1965, pp. 847–52.

crop diversification. This trend was continued into a second phase by the substitution of tractors for mules, herbicides for hoes, and machines for cotton-pickers. The sustained civil rights and political attacks upon the Jim Crow system of white supremacy facilitated the mobility of southern blacks. The pull of the city has primarily been exerted through wartime labor shortages. World War I occasioned the first massive migration to the North. The restriction of European immigration in 1924 created a semipermanent niche for blacks to become the new recruits into the pool of unskilled labor, which frequently became surplus labor. Successive demands for workers in World War II, the Korean War, and the Vietnam War have repeated the pattern. The North had other attractions—higher wages, better hours, and a system of racial controls less obvious than the South's Jim Crow.

The population movement was not confined to the North alone, for it also involved a general shift to urban areas within the South. This internal migration from countryside to city is of major importance, although too often it has been ignored because it was overshadowed by the regional shifts. As the southern population becomes more demographically similar to the northern population, the nature of racism in both regions is beginning to assume greater similarities, especially in metropolitan centers.

Before World War II, the racial practices of the cities within the border states were more akin to those of cities in the South. Since the United States Supreme Court struck down *de jure* segregation in the *Brown* decision of 1954, the border cities have become much more similar to northern cities. Today it is difficult to distinguish the racial practices in the border metropolises, such as St. Louis and Baltimore, from their counterparts in the North. With the Supreme Court's repeated reinforcement of its rulings on the unconstitutionality of Jim Crow laws and the passage of federal legislation to support these procedures, the institutional forms of the racial systems of the larger southern metropolitan areas, such as Atlanta and Dallas, are rapidly becoming similar to those of the border cities. The roles have changed and the South is now taking lessons from the North in matters of race.

THE STRUCTURE OF URBAN RACISM: A MODEL

The legal code that made the slave system and its successor the Jim Crow system so clear-cut is no longer the shaper of urban racism—North or South. In fact, much of the North has been without segregation laws for almost a century, and today antidiscrimination laws are common for housing, employment, and public accommodations. Within public and private organizations, many of the formal, and even the informal, unstated rules on race have been dropped or modified. Nevertheless, the social institutions have adapted to their historic heritage. Urban racism shows no sign of disappearing and operates almost as if it were sanctioned by statute.

Under these conditions urban racism defies concise definition. It is accurately definable only in terms of its diffusion throughout the operation of the major sectors of metropolitan life and through the procedures by which important institutions of the city establish priorities and choose between competing objectives. The immediate racial barriers, although they are still strong, do not, *per se,* define urban racism. In fact, within any particular institutional sector of urban life, the racial barriers have numerous fuzzy edges and exceptions. Many organizations which excluded blacks two years ago are now avidly seeking some token black representation. The effectiveness of urban racism is dependent upon the manner in which the racial controls and differentiation in one institutional sector fit together to reinforce the distinctions in other sectors. As the specific barriers become less distinctive and less absolute, their meshing together into an overriding network compensates, so that the combined effect of the whole is greater than the sum of the individual institutions. The minute operations of these institutions are so interrelated and bolster one another so efficiently they form a coherent system of control without the sanction of a legal framework.

Maintenance of the basic racial controls is now less dependent upon specific discriminatory decisions. Such behavior has become so well institutionalized that the individual generally does not have to exercise a choice to operate in a racist manner. The rules and procedures of the large organizations have already prestructured the choice. The individual only has to conform to the operating norms of the organization and the institution will do the discriminating for him.

Our model of urban racism has two major conceptual components regarding institutional structures: 1) Within the major institutional networks that operate in the city there have developed definable black subsectors which operate on a subordinated basis, subject to the advantage, control, and priorities of the dominant systems. 2) A circular pattern of reinforcement takes place between the barriers that define the various black subsectors. A third component regarding power and stability of the entire urban system is essential to our model; but since this deals more with modes of operation than institutional structures, we leave any treatment of this topic to the later section on "Maintaining the Balance."

The major institutional sectors whose operation and mutual reinforcement provide the basic sinews for the system of racial controls are the housing market and its related field of planning, the labor market, the educational system, and the political structure with the welfare system it controls.

In each of these institutional areas, there has developed historically a dual system of operations in which there is a dominant white system and a subordinate black subsystem. The well established adaptation of both racial groups to these institutional dualities makes it possible to perpetuate such divisions, even though the absolute color line between the subdivisions might not be as strong in specific cases as they once were. This line is infrequently tested, for blacks as a group operate in the black subsector and whites as a group operate in the white subsector. Discrimination and discouragement usually remain sufficiently strong to prevent too many from operating out of their own area. Deliberate exclusion of the large magnitude that was necessary originally to create the subordinate black subsectors is no longer requisite for their perpetuation.

The fact that the black subsectors exist on a subordinated basis is necessary to make the mutual reinforcement among sectors effective. These subsectors have become the primary basis upon which the racial distinctions are institutionally structured. The second-class outcomes for blacks from any one institutional sector are so strong and enduring because the subordinated subsectors provide concrete organizational forms and procedures which can be bolstered. It is not just attitudes or individually controlled behavior that are reinforced.

In order to have a discriminatory effect, criteria, rules, and procedures within any single organization may now be much less based on race. The racial distinctions and differentiations created in any one institutional area operate as instruments supporting the segregation and unequal treatment that take place in the other institutions. An organization's procedures can be based upon the outcomes of some other institutional operation. These outcomes might not have a racial label but nonetheless have a high racial correlation. A few examples: the school system uses the neighborhood-school policy which, combined with residential segregation, operates as a surrogate for direct segregation; suburbs in creating very restrictive zoning regulations, or urban-renewal developments in setting universally high rents, can eliminate all but a very few black families on the basis of income; given the racial differentials produced by the school system, an employer, by using his regular personnel tests and criteria, can screen out most blacks from desirable jobs.

If any single institution, say the school system or the labor market, maintained its present form of operation alone, outside the web of urban racism, its efficiency in racial differentiation would greatly diminish. This is not to say that explicit racial barriers and discrimination no longer exist; it does say that once the fundamental institutional relationships have been established, overtly exclusionary barriers become less important for the overall oppressive functioning of the system of urban racism.

The seemingly impersonal institutions of the great cities have been woven together into a web of urban racism that entraps black people much as the spider's net holds flies—they can wiggle but they cannot move very far. There is a carefully articulated interrelation of the barriers created by each institution. Whereas the single institutional strand standing alone might not be so strong, the many strands together form a powerful web. But here the analogy breaks down. In contrast to the spider's prey, the victim of urban racism has fed on stronger stuff and is on the threshold of tearing the web.

This spreading out of the racial controls through such a variety of institutional forms, plus the ideological distortions in the way that they have been viewed, make it difficult to discern the actual social structure that makes urban racism operational. From within the black community it tends to appear that there is just a massive white sea that surrounds a black island. The further down one is on the ladder of status and income, the more this view prevails. To white liberals and sophisticated managers in business and government, urban race relations has the appearance of being a number of problems, related somewhat through the life cycle of blacks. They view the problems as basically soluble through spending more resources on the accepted techniques of social and business management.

At one time it was popular to claim that the environment of the northern city was antithetical to racism. Rural black peasants, it was held, would just need a generation or two to acculturate into the urban melting pot. After all, were they not just the newest immigrants—a kind of black Irishmen? The hard evidence holds to the contrary—racism's roots now are firmly embedded in the urban environment. The major population shift has had little effect on the basic socioeconomic position of blacks vis-à-vis whites in the cities. The racial gap in social benefits is basically not being closed, even in a period of unprecedented prosperity. The Vietnam War is having less of an effect in improving blacks' incomes and occupations than did World War II. In the slum areas of the large cities the number of poor blacks has remained constant since 1960. Truly, the city must have its own technique for locking blacks in. An accurate historic or analytic view can leave no doubt that the functioning of the system still involves a perpetuation of segregation, subordination, subjugation, and exploitation.

What remains to be clarified is the nature of the social structures by which these relations are maintained. In the examination of the individual sectors, most of the ideas and a good deal of the evidence were developed from studies of Chicago. The picture in its broad outlines, however, holds for all major metropolitan areas.

The Dual Labor Market and Employment Discrimination

When we consider the black man in the city's economy, his role is basically confined to that of being the employee and the consumer. In other words, in this capitalistic economy black people are cut off from the sources of power, wealth, and influence that come from the control of corporate enterprises. In a society such as ours where wealth and ownership are the most enduring sources of power, such exclusion will limit the strength and opportunities of a group in many noneconomic areas of the society and is a major element in defining the constraints of racism. In terms of the economy itself, however, this means that we can comprehend the black man's basic role when we consider him as a seller of labor in the job market.

A racial dualism in the metropolitan labor markets provides the structure that determines such different results for blacks and whites. In practice, the metropolitan labor market consists of two sectors: a primary job market in which firms recruit white workers and white workers look for jobs, and a smaller secondary market in which firms recruit black workers and black workers look for jobs. There are distinct sets of demand and supply forces determining earnings and occupational distribution in each for the white and black sectors of the job market; the two sectors also differ as to practices and procedures for the recruitment, hiring, training, and promotion of workers. Labor market studies indicate that the black jobseeker is quite the rational economic man in confronting his realistic opportunities. Therefore, we must conclude that these vastly different racial results came about because the black worker faces a very differently structured set of opportunities. In effect, certain jobs have become designated as "Negro" jobs. Black workers are hired by certain industries, by particular firms within these industries, and for particular jobs within these firms. Within all industries, including government service, there is unmistakable evidence of occupational ceilings for blacks. Within establishments that hire both blacks and whites, the black workers are usually limited to specific job classifications and production units. An accurate rule of thumb is that the lower the pay or the more disagreeable and dirty the job the greater the chance of finding a high proportion of Negroes.

Within the racial division of the labor market, the black subsector clearly is in a subordinate position. Jobs are distributed between white and black workers in a way that gives white workers the first opportunity for employment. Expansion of employment opportunities for the black workers occurs only during periods of tight labor markets when certain jobs transfer either partially or fully from the white to the black subsector. Most firms actively recruit black workers only when the pool of white labor is drying up. Furthermore, black workers are concentrated in marginal or declining industries and firms. Under these conditions, a large part of the black labor force forms a pool of surplus labor that is excluded from the normal functioning of the economy.

Historically, wartime tight labor markets have provided the occasions when the surplus labor reserve of black workers has been drawn upon. In subsequent peacetime slackening of labor demand, discrimination has operated to ration off the smaller number of jobs to the white man's advantage and to wipe out most of the relative gains made by the black man. During times of labor scarcity individual firms might drastically change their personnel policies, hiring black workers where none had been employed before or upgrading them into positions that were previously lily-white. Such a process was first instituted during World War I and has been repeated with every succeeding war. The new black workers were recruited from the surplus labor of the rural South and from the unemployed and underemployed in the urban ghettoes. Today, since there are relatively few black people left in rural areas, the city provides the major portion of the black surplus labor reserve.

The effects of this dual labor market structure is revealed in the position in the urban economy of black workers vis-à-vis white workers. During the last twenty years of general prosperity their relative standings have remained remarkably stable. Both groups have improved their incomes and upgraded their occupations, but the rate of improvement for blacks has been insufficient to diminish their proportionate distance behind whites. Economic growth and shifts in the occupational mix during this period have provided conditions for the economic assimilation of other groups. Indeed, if blacks faced barriers in the labor market that were similar to those faced by immigrant ethnic groups, there would have been a remarkable shift in their relative status. The grim facts speak differently. The incomes of black workers and families, when considered on a nationwide basis, have basically remained at a constant percentage of white incomes since World War II. The ratio has fluctuated around 55 per cent—falling as low as 51 per cent in peacetime and rising higher during the Korean and Vietnamese wars. The national figures hide the effect of wage improvement caused by migration out of the South, for in every region the income gap for black males increased in the decade 1950–60. Black women have somewhat improved their positions.[9]

Unemployment is falling harder on the black worker now than it did right after World War II. The black unemployment rate has increased from a little over one and a half times the white rate in 1948 to over twice the white rate in the mid-1950's. Today, in the major cities, the black unemployment rate is two and a half to four times that of the whites. For Chicago, the latest figures indicate white unemployment at 2.3 per cent of the civilian labor force and black unemployment at 7.6 per cent.

Racial differences in unemployment rates and income are only partially explainable on the basis of differences in education and occupation. In every occupational group and at every level of education, black workers have higher unemployment rates and lower incomes than whites with comparable backgrounds. Studies that take into account variation in education, occupation, and other relevant characteristics have found that between 13 and 38 per cent of the differential between the incomes of black and white men is attributable to discrimination.[10] Even unskilled workers are penal-

---

[9] Alan Batchelder, "The Decline in the Relative Income of Negro Men," *Quarterly Journal of Economics,* Vol. 78 (November, 1964), 525–48. For measurement of the occupational gap see Gary Becker, *The Economics of Discrimination* (Chicago: University of Chicago Press, 1957), pp. 112–13, and Herman Miller, *Rich Man, Poor Man* (New York: Thomas Y. Crowell, 1964), pp. 99–103.

[10] James M. Morgan, *et al., Income and Welfare in the United States* (New York: McGraw-Hill, Inc., 1962), p. 56, and Paul M. Siegel, "On the Cost of Being a Negro," *Sociological Inquiry,* Vol. 35 (Winter, 1965), 41–57.

ized solely on the basis of race. In Chicago, during 1964, black material handlers received 32 cents an hour less than whites of comparable training and background; black janitors received 10 cents an hour less.[11]

As a result of the extended economic boom, the wartime tight labor market and the changes in public and private policies brought about by the civil rights movement, it is true that a top group of younger, better-trained black workers have improved their conditions enough in the last half dozen years to narrow the gap a little between themselves and their white counterparts. A middle group of approximately one half of the black workers has managed to share tenuously in the prosperity by maintaining its same relative position in regard to whites. However, even the extremely favorable current conditions have not been able to neutralize the effects of urban racism on the one third or more of the families in the cities that constitute the black underclass.

For those blacks trapped in the slum sectors of the ghetto, the United States Department of Labor concludes that "social and economic conditions are getting worse, not better." This group is not only falling further behind the whites, but they were better off eight years ago before the long boom started. In the Hough section of Cleveland, black families in 1965 had $800 less in real purchasing power than they had in 1960; in South Los Angeles, family purchasing power fell off by $200. Unemployment rates in these areas, even during a boom, generally range upwards of 10 per cent. Regular unemployment rates, however, do not represent the real conditions of the black underclass. Accordingly, the Department of Labor in a special study developed the category of *subemployed*, which includes the underemployed and the discouraged workers who have dropped out of the labor force altogether. For nine major slum areas across the country in 1966 they found that one of three adult males was subemployed.[12] Only in the subsequent two years with the increased tempo of the economy due to the Vietnam War has there been a slight reversal of this downward trend.

[11] David P. Taylor, *The Unskilled Negro Worker in the Chicago Labor Market* (Chicago: Chicago Urban League, 1967).
[12] U.S. Department of Labor, *Manpower Report of the President, 1967*, pp. 73–91.

Housing and Land Planning

The stark reality of the urban ghettoes eliminates the need for citing elaborate statistics to prove the existence of residential segregation and racially dual housing markets.[13] The United States Bureau of the Census shows that segregation within cities and the current concentration of the black population in central cities have *increased* during the sixties.[14]

The existence of separate housing markets—one for whites and another for blacks—is provable by a study of the operations of the market institutions and by measurement of differentials in market results. Overwhelmingly, real estate brokers refuse to show blacks properties outside the ghetto or transition neighborhoods. Lending institutions refuse to grant them mortgages for properties beyond these confines. Blacks are restricted to considering purchase or lease only of those units which come on the black market. In turn, whites, because of prejudice and a realistic recognition of the worse conditions in the ghetto, limit their shopping to properties in the white market.

Comparable housing units have different prices depending upon the racial sector in which they are located. Since blacks have a restricted supply of housing and a growing demand, they have to pay a premium or a "color tax." An Urban League study for Chicago shows that for rental units, which comprise four-fifths of the black

[13] As Karl and Alma Taeuber concluded after their exhaustive study,

> In the urban United States, there is a very high degree of segregation of the residences of whites and Negroes. This is true for cities in all regions of the country and for all types of cities—large and small, industrial and commercial, metropolitan and suburban. It is true whether there are hundreds of thousands of Negro residents, or only a few thousand. Residential segregation prevails regardless of the relative economic status of the white and Negro residents. It occurs regardless of the character of local laws and policies, and regardless of the extent of other forms of segregation or discrimination.

Karl E. and Alma F. Taeuber, *Negroes in Cities* (Chicago: Aldine Publishing Company, 1965), pp. 35–36.

[14] "Negro Population: March 1966," *Current Population Reports,* Series P-20, No. 168.

housing, blacks pay 10 per cent more than whites for comparable units. Rapkin, in examining regional and national data, shows systematic patterns of price discrimination against black renters.[15]

Regardless of social or economic status, almost all blacks are locked into the ghetto. Because of the perpetual housing shortage, all social strata in the black community have to pay more for their dwellings. All sections of the ghetto are subject to manipulation which ignores their interests in matters of zoning and land planning. But the worst off are the poor who are locked into the slums. Cut-up apartments, negligent landlords, and inefficient public services characterize these areas. The ghetto is bad not because it is inhabited by black people, but because it is operated as a subjected enclave. The will and interests of others than the inhabitants rule over the black neighborhoods. The ghetto, in this restrictive sense, is not a free community; it is the product of oppression.

At the beginning of this century, the black housing enclaves were no more segregated than the areas in which many of the European immigrant groups lived. However, the immigrant groups dispersed, while the blacks became more segregated. Rigid policing of the ghetto walls was largely organized in the period right after World War I by the real estate industry through restrictive covenants and control of mortgage funds. The encouragement of violence was not unknown. People became conditioned to participating in the housing market along specific racial lines so that even when restrictive covenants were declared unenforceable, the old patterns endured.

A second phase in the shoring up of the ghetto came about after World War II. Urban planning and redevelopment became the major new instruments for keeping black areas subordinated and consolidated during this period. Urban renewal to improve the environment of prestigious institutions and expressway construction to make the city accessible to the suburbanites, displaced many of the families in the ghetto and further diminished an already limited black housing supply. New construction of public housing was so

[15] Chester Rapkin, "Price Discrimination Against Negroes in the Rental Housing Market," in *Essays in Urban Economics, In Honor of the Birthday of Leo Goebler* (Los Angeles: University of California, 1966), pp. 333–42.

located as to keep many of the displaced black families within the already established ghettoes.

The urban ghettoes are increasingly isolated from the majority of the new jobs located in the suburban ring. Transportation is inadequate and costly. Furthermore, the large size and homogeneity of the black areas makes it easy to develop segregated school systems on the basis of neighborhood policies.

Education

Educational systems have become a major pillar of racism, precisely because education has become so important in the total scheme of our society. The sophistication of the technology employed in the economy makes educational achievement a prerequisite for a decent job. In 1900, when only 6 per cent of the youth in the nation graduated from high school and unskilled jobs abounded, the urban school systems were not a major instrumentality in creating racial distinctions. Today, when over 70 per cent of all youths graduate from high school and over 50 per cent of the graduates go on to some kind of college, educational institutions which provide markedly different results for black and white children are key to the structure of urban racism. Next to the family, they are the most important institutional molder of the child in our society.

Without the support of any statutory provisions, urban school systems operate very efficiently on a *de facto* racially segregated basis. This segregation invariably occurs where racial groups are residentially segregated and there is a neighborhood school policy. In the past, many boards of education have gerrymandered school boundaries and used various student transfer policies so as to create all-black or all-white schools. Civil rights pressures have put an end to most of these maneuvers. Nevertheless, with the large size and the homogeneity of the ghettoes, no special policies are needed to maintain Jim Crow schools today.

In the larger cities, there are, in effect, two school subsystems—one for blacks and one for whites. These subsystems help define both a spacial and social distance between the two racial groups. In Chicago, for instance, conclusive evidence shows that the extent of racial segregation has been increasing in recent years: in 1965, 90 per cent of the black elementary and 72 per cent of the black high school pupils attended schools that were virtually all black. Six of the public school systems in the ten largest cities had 89 per cent or more of their black pupils in schools that were 90 to 100 per cent black. Even in many of the schools that have bi-racial student bodies, homogeneous groupings and track systems often create a high degree of internal segregation.

As in the case of the other areas of urban life, the status and conditions of the black sub-sectors of the urban school systems are distinctly inferior. Usually, they are located in the central cities which spend less per pupil than the better-off suburbs. The second-class nature of the black section of the city school system can be measured in terms of both the inputs and outputs of the system. In the black schools, the board of education maintains larger classroom size, has a lower per pupil expenditure, concentrates its teacher shortage, is less sensitive to the expressed needs of the community, and has lower expectations for both the pupils and faculties. These lesser inputs are matched by comparable results. By the sixth grade, black pupils have average achievement levels that lag two years behind those of white pupils; this lag increases to more than three years in the higher grades. Moreover, the black pupils incorporate in their own self-images much of the low esteem with which the school system holds them. It should be noted that during the last few years, in response to the pressures of the civil rights movement and with federal grants in aid, there has been some increase in the inputs into the black sub-sectors so that the disparities are no longer so great within the central city. Since the racial differentials in educational inputs constitute only one element of the total system, the net effect of any equalizing of expenditures has been to keep the disparity in educational results from increasing. Further, in spite of any more equitable distribution of educational funds between racial groups as a whole, a recent study of public school expenditures in the Chicago metropolitan area shows that the high-status whites have been able to increase the amounts spent on their children at a faster rate than any other group, black or white. While racial advantage in this regard might be narrowing, class advantage is growing.

Education has traditionally been conceived of as one of the great ladders of social mobility within our society. Presently, for the average black child in the ghetto, the school operates more as an instrument of subjugation than liberation. The subordination of the black sector in these vast training systems conditions the individual black youngster to expect a subordinate position for the rest of his life. The involvement of both black and white youth for twelve years in a segregated system creates in them the expectation that a certain amount of segregation is normal. The atmosphere and curriculum in the classroom reinforces the equally false, but socially powerful, sense of superiority in white pupils and sense of inferiority in black pupils through the nature of the textual materials and the attitudes of the staff. The smaller financial and technological inputs into the black subsectors have meant preferential treatment for white pupils in the allocation of public resources. The racial differentials in standard educational results have meant the rationing out of a smaller proportion of the favorable life and occupational opportunities to the black pupils.

Political Structure

For the last hundred years in the northern cities, and much more recently in the southern cities, the black citizen has had the franchise. He has used it skillfully, but having to operate in narrow confines, he has not been able to gain much actual power. Contrary to some mythology, he does not neglect to exercise his voting rights in those places where he is not barred from the ballot box. In the North and West, differences in registering and voting between whites and blacks, in proportion to the voting age population, are small—only a few percentage points apart. In the presidential election of 1964, 72 per cent of the blacks and 75 per cent of the whites voted in those sections. The disparity is so small that it can be explained in terms of differentials in such nonracial factors as education, occupation, and income.[16] Though there might not be

[16] Angus Campbell, *et al., The American Voter* (New York: John Wiley and Sons, 1966), p. 282.

much difference in respect to what the black man as a citizen puts into the political system, there is a vast difference in what he gets out of it.

The black political leadership or organization operates as a dependent element in the larger party organization and government administration. Since the New Deal days, blacks have overwhelmingly supported the Democratic party. Black politicians have become a minor ally in the councils of that party. In no sense are they major voices in setting the party's course at either local or national levels. The form and style of black politicians is dependent upon the nature of the local political structures within which they operate. In the case of Chicago, where there is a strong Democratic party organization and a powerful black section of the party, James Wilson makes the point that the black organization's strength and cohesiveness is largely dependent upon the strength and cohesiveness of the overall county organization—it is "a 'sub-machine' within a larger city-wide machine." [17] This relationship is so structured that the black politicians cannot use their considerable electoral strength for important policy ends.

Black officeholders almost invariably come from electoral districts with a black majority among the voters. In ten of the largest non-southern cities, only two—Cleveland and Los Angeles—have greater representation for blacks in the city council than their proportion of the total population. For most of these cities, the council representation is about one half the proportion of the black percentage in the total population.[18] Despite the fact that blacks are represented in city governments, in no large city do the black councilmen have enough real power to act as a strong veto block on major issues. The election of black mayors in Gary and Cleveland might change this factor in those cities. However, increasing dependence of urban budgets upon federal programs and grants-in-aid might mitigate the actual importance of these shifts in power.

On citywide boards and judicial slates that are elected at-large

[17] James Q. Wilson, *Negro Politics, The Search for Leadership* (Glencoe, Illinois: The Free Press, 1960), p. 26b.

[18] James Q. Wilson, "The Negro in American Politics: The Present," in John P. Davis, ed., *The American Negro Reference Book* (Englewood Cliffs, New Jersey: Prentice-Hall, Inc., 1966), p. 444.

or appointed by the chief executive, black representatives are often included to balance the slate. Many times this is a token representative who is a weak man chosen because a black is required to legitimate, but not direct, the decisions of the board or agency.

The subordinate and second-class status of the urban black political operation is revealed in the minor influence that black people have on major political decisions. The lack of influence over important issues is reflected in the small number of blacks in top administrative positions which control policy. Another Chicago example shows that in 1965, blacks held 7 out of 50 aldermanic positions, but they only held 2 out of the 156 top appointive policy-making posts in the city administration. Within these kinds of constraints, present-day black political activity must be judged as a strategy of limited objectives. To turn to James Wilson again:

> Where Negroes can and do vote, they have it in their power to end the indifference or hostility of their elected representatives, but the representatives do not have it in their power to alter fundamentally the lot of the Negro. The vote is a legally important, morally essential weapon for the protection and advancement of individual and group interests but it cannot protect or advance *all* the relevant interests. It can force the passage of laws, the ending of obvious forms of state-sanctioned discrimination, and the removal from office of race-baiters and avowed segregationists. It can only marginally effect the income, housing, occupation or life chances of Negro electorates.[19]

If power is construed in a quasi-political sense that extends beyond the formal structure of government and recognizes the great influence of other large organizations, we can see that the power of the black man is even more constricted. In this sense the powerlessness of blacks has been maintained by their exclusion from positions of authority in white-controlled institutions and by narrowly hemming in black-controlled institutions. Exclusion from policy posts in the dominant sectors has been enforced primarily by unwritten "white-only" policies. For those few blacks who do get into such posts, the pressures are great to conform to the established norms of second-class treatment for the mass of black people.

[19] *Ibid.,* p. 456.

A recent Chicago Urban League study documents the extent of black exclusion from decision-making structures for the Chicago area. Out of some 11,000 positions in Cook County that were vested with a policy-making potential within major public and private institutions, it was found that blacks occupied 2.6 per cent of these posts, although they constituted 20 per cent of the county's population. When actual power was estimated by weighing the kinds of positions occupied and analyzing how Negroes were able to function within them, it was shown that less than 1 per cent of the effective power was wielded by blacks. Where black representation did occur, it was primarily through the influence of a black constituency, especially when that constituency had electoral powers, as in public and trade union offices. Business firms, accordingly, had the whitest control structure of any sector.

Within the established channels of the institutions of the dominant society, blacks are virtually powerless. Within the major institutional sectors of housing, employment, politics, and education, blacks in posts of authority were almost universally confined to places within the black subsector. (Whites may occupy some of the more lucrative and prestigious positions even here.) The influence of these individuals is circumscribed by the basic subordination of the subsector within which they operate. In other words, the legitimate limits to their exercise of power are bound by the condition that they do not basically disturb the balance of the dominant society. Therefore, influence vis-à-vis the dominant sector is usually confined to getting minor concessions.

Low incomes, lowly occupations, and the lack of significant ownership do not provide blacks with the type of prestige that commands influence in the political arena. Their opposition to a project can be overrun: for example, it is easier to condemn large tracts of land in order to run an expressway through a poor black community than to do the same in a white community. The levers of power that come from the control of other large organizations are not available to black people for shaping of decisions. Even in gaining the spoils of office, blacks come off second best. What Gosnell wrote of black politicians thirty years ago still holds true today: "The political organizations of the group were not in a position to benefit from the most lucrative varieties of political graft that had been common in Chicago. There were no great Negro contracting firms, no Negro banks that did a city-wide business, no Negro real estate men that operated on a county-wide basis, and no Negroes in the administrative posts that furnished the greatest opportunity for the spoils." [20]

The fact that such a high proportion of the black population is dependent on public welfare for its income (almost one out of four blacks in Chicago and one out of seven nationally) and on public housing for its shelter greatly inhibits the exercise of political influence for long-run gains. These persons are treated as outcasts and are stigmatized by the larger society. The bureaucratic machinery to which they relate handles them like wards of the state, rather than responsible adults. The conditions of their survival impose a powerlessness upon them and deprives them of political influence.

What black political strength that does exist often concerns itself with meeting the immediate needs of the black poor. For these concessions, their long-run interests are often sacrificed. For example, where urban renewal creates a housing shortage for black families, their politicians might use their influence to get more public housing at the cost of accepting inadequate project design and locating them in impractical areas of existing ghettoes. Such locations further increase segregation and add additional burdens to already overused community resources. Some black politicians and administrators have become specialized to this type of operation. Because they meet immediate needs, they make their constituents dependent on them and survive in office.

Of course, there are those traditional organizations that are primarily of the black community rather than part of some metropolitanwide institutional network. Such organizations tend to be religious, social, or fraternal in nature; therefore, they are not the kind of structures that wield much power within this society. Further, their long-run continuance has generally been dependent upon some mode of accommodation with the general racial system. The organization that tests the controls too strongly is punished by harassment or withdrawal of support. Accordingly, the traditional influentials in the black community have been forced to

[20] Harold Gosnell, *Negro Politicians: The Rise of Negro Politics in Chicago* (Chicago: University of Chicago Press, 1935, 1966), pp. 364–65.

assume a position within which they have a certain amount of influence and control in their own milieu in return for not upsetting the basic controls of the dominant society.

Perhaps the real racial limitations and restrictions within the standard political framework are best evidenced by the reactions to them within the black community and the forms which social action is taking there. As black people increasingly demand the overthrow of racial oppression no matter what guise it takes, there has been a concomitant disillusionment with the effectiveness of the usual American political processes of incremental adjustments and the compromising of interests as means of achieving these ends. These marginal rearrangements only allow the established systems to find new modes for asserting their dominance. As a result there has been a growth of nationalistically oriented organizations and program planning. And the essence of nationalism is to assert a new basis for sovereignty and legitimacy. Black power is in effect a rhetorical manifestation of this development. While not all users of this slogan go so far as to seek a new basis for political legitimacy, at minimum they do find it necessary to line themselves up symbolically with the deeply felt assessment that for the black man the present political system basically operates as an instrument of subjugation rather than an instrument of representation.

So far we have discussed lack of power in the context of exclusion from political and institutional leadership. Other aspects of black powerlessness operate in individual lives. The struggle for survival within the confines of racism saps one's strength. "The ghetto," as Kenneth Clark tells us, "fails to prepare one for voluntary sacrifices precisely because it demands so many involuntary ones." [21] For the poor the power to control personal day-to-day affairs is often denied. The welfare systems and the housing authorities function as if the adults who receive their services are their wards. An administrative manual and a case worker supervise lives of recipients to the point of having to give approval on both the purchase of a bed and the use of the bed once it is paid for. The bureaucratic structures operate on the assumption that if you are poor, especially poor and black, you are not capable of regulating your own affairs.

[21] Kenneth Clark, *Dark Ghetto, Dilemmas of Social Power* (New York: Harper & Row, Inc., 1965), p. 189.

The Pieces Fall in Place

The lines that functionally define the black subsectors in the major institutions are effectively linked together. The black man's career in any one subordinate subsector establishes preconditions for him to get inferior results from any other sector. Therefore, the actual racial discrimination in a particular institution need not be as great as the differential in its racial outcome, for the other institutional sectors have previously performed much of the discrimination for it.

The ghetto provides the base for the segregated schools. The inferior education in ghetto schools handicaps the black worker in the labor market. Employment discrimination causes low wages and frequent unemployment. Low incomes limit the market choices of black families in housing. Lack of education, low level occupations, and exclusion from ownership or control of large enterprises inhibit the development of political power. The lack of political power prevents black people from changing basic housing, planning and educational programs. Each sector strengthens the racial subordination in the rest of the urban institutions.

THE TRADITION OF RACISM IN THE NEW MILIEU

In describing the operation of racism in the present-day urban environment, we have, up to this point, concentrated on one particular perspective. The conceptual framework has emphasized the existence of dependent, subordinate black subsectors within the major institutional sectors of metropolitan society. These subsectors are functionally well defined even though there are no clear-cut laws or rules which delineate them. The racial functions of the different institutional sectors reinforce one another—for whites, dominance in one sector reinforces dominance in another—for blacks, subordination in one sector reinforces subordination in another. Therefore, through this process of mutual support, these systems can continue operating with day-to-day procedures that are largely color-blind. This kind of abstraction was used to make the unique elements of modern racism stand out in bold relief. Now, let us retrace our steps to see how the more traditional elements of racism as a caste-like system operate within this new structure. These traditional factors provide the glue which holds the institutional web of racism together.

Norms

It cannot be denied that individual attitudes and prejudices are significant for perpetuating racial discrimination, but in order to understand racism as an institutional phenomenon, it is necessary to view individual behavior in terms of norms and roles.

Given the prevalence of racism and its supporting ideology, every major institution in this society functions on the basis that some amount, usually a lot, of racial subordination is *normal*. If it is not openly considered to be good, it is at least expected and held to be unavoidable. As an example, the educational system accepts as normal that black pupils should have a markedly lower performance in academic skills. The norms of an organization are, in effect, its standards of achievement. They are the guideposts which tell an individual what is expected of him by an institution and what he can expect of the institution. White Americans assume black inferiority. An institution is considered to be functioning properly if it provides inferior results from blacks.

Once a racial norm is established in a particular social area, it tends to endure. The elaborate institutional mechanisms and explicit policies that were necessary to bring norms into being are no longer necessary to keep them functional. A far lesser amount of reinforcement will maintain the effectiveness of the norm. As an illustration: the racial duality in the housing markets is particularly dependent upon the different expectations that whites and blacks have in the marketplace. Legally enforced restrictive covenants, federal government regulations, and discriminatory codes for the banking and real estate industries were among the means necessary to construct two separate markets with their two different sets of norms. These formal discriminatory measures have now been canceled or made less blatant without much real change taking place.

In spite of these changes, the two markets are well enough established on their own to maintain the old norms without extraordinary measures. Most shifts in policy, in reality, have produced modification and amelioration of the racial norms, rather than wiping out their superordinate-subordinate prescriptions. In other words, the effect of the antidiscrimination and equal opportunity policies to date has been to create a situation in which a little less discrimination is considered normal.

Roles

Conformity to norms is basically perpetuated by inculcating the roles of an institution within the individual. "Impulse and sensitivity are channeled and transformed into standard motives joined to standard goals and gratifications. Thus, institutions imprint their stamps upon the individual, modifying his external conduct as well as his inner life." Roles, therefore, "may be segments of various institutions and at the same time components of persons." [22] The acting out of a role in a stable organization tends to become habitual so that the individual does not constantly have to judge whether he is conforming to the established norms. Under such conditions, while there will be a range of variation among individuals, role performances usually will conform to role expectations.

An institution in which racial discrimination and subordination are normal maintains its stability by specifying different roles for white and black. In regard to the major white-controlled institutions, the black's role is supposed to be one of submission and patience, with limited aspiration and motivation. Whites, too, learn racial roles which prescribe that no matter what subordination he owes to persons in positions of control, he should expect deference from blacks and preference over them. [23] Urban school systems function as extremely efficient training institutions for the development of racial roles. The Caucasian child will be instructed and

[22] Hans Gerth and C. Wright Mills, *Character and Social Structure, the Psychology of Social Institutions* (New York: Harcourt, Brace & World, Inc., 1963), pp. 109–73.
[23] For an extended discussion of racial roles, see Thomas F. Pettigrew, *A Profile of the Negro American* (Princeton: D. Van Nostrand Co., 1964).

motivated as to the manner and style that society expects of him as a superordinate "white," while the black child will be likewise trained as a subordinate "Negro."

The joint forces of all institutions in which the individual significantly interacts create what can be considered as a generalized role vis-à-vis the entire society. In terms of the individual, it becomes an element of personality that is carried from one situation or institution to another. While this generalized role is basically what makes racism so consistent, it can be segmented into somewhat different, and even contradictory, roles in the various settings within which the individual operates. For example, the same white workers can function on a cooperative basis with blacks in a trade union, even electing them to high office, and then in a housing context violently deny blacks' right to freedom of residence. Or a white executive can operate deferentially to blacks in the course of a race relations luncheon, and yet proceed to discriminate with ease when he returns to his office. A black man can be a submissive, obeisant porter in a bank during the day and go home to the ghetto at night to become a respected official in his church.[24]

As another aspect of role segmentation, it is possible for a black to fill a management or professional role in a racist manner that is little different from his white counterpart's. A classic example of this process is the middle-class black teacher who inculcates her lower-status black charges with the idea that they are unteachable. The basic institutional pressures operate in this direction, for the individual is constrained to conform to the given norms and role expectations of the organization that confers status upon him, i.e., they are expected to treat other blacks according to the established patterns.

Today, the concepts of "black pride" and "black consciousness" are creating a revolution in the role expectations of high school and college students. Youth in the ghetto are projecting patterns of behavior and action which are totally at variance with the traditional role of "Negro" as deferential and dependent. At this stage, these new self-concepts are being defined on the basis of black

[24] See Thomas F. Pettigrew, "Complexity and Change in American Racial Patterns: A Social and Psychological View," *Daedalus,* Fall, 1965, pp. 974–79.

solidarity and only secondarily on blacks' relationships to whites. Therefore, this new generalized role that is emerging is not only in conflict with the particular role of blacks in any specific organization, but it is also at variance with the idea of a black filling a supervisory or high-status role in the same manner as the traditional "white" role. The development of these new role concepts will bring the black youth into conflict with the racist norms and methods of operation in our major institutions. The form of this conflict will depend upon the social, economic, and political strategies that are utilized to create new structural arrangements in which the new role of the liberated black man can be made concrete in specific institutional roles.

Class

Many of the points that have been made about norms, roles, and power apply in some degree to all persons who are poor and of low status, regardless of color. Class provides another dimension within which American society parcels out life chances. While class lines, in the sense of status graduations, are much less rigid than racial lines, they are significant to the point of largely determining the limits of one's career and the careers of one's children. The upper and middle classes are provided with greater service benefits, such as investment in their children's education. They are accorded deference and access to preferred places on the basis of having acquired the style of their group. Their influence in community decisions is greater than their proportionate numbers. The needs and interests of the lower classes are usually subordinated to those of greater status. Such preference is legitimized by being considered right and naturally belonging to those who have a stake in the social order.

Historically, blacks have been relegated to the bottom of the status ladder. Slavery soon defined a class to which only persons of African ancestry belonged. With the abolition of slavery, rural tenancy became the bottom status and it was shared with poor whites. Class distinctions did begin to develop within the black community with the growth of a small professional class and a smaller business class. This class structure, even in the modern urban setting, is a truncated one. Today, blacks are virtually excluded from corporate proprietorship and management, which is the major determinant of high and controlling status in American society. By and large, they do not even have the kinds of ownership, occupations, incomes, or education which confer the lesser but still advantageous social ranks. Since blacks are much more concentrated at the lower status levels than are whites, the present hierarchical class structure operates in addition to race as a means of reinforcing the subordinate position of blacks.

In the post-World War II period, the norm of white America has been a middle-class one; i.e., unless there was clear evidence to the opposite, in a specified situation, every white is considered to have a middle-class life style. He is, therefore, given the deference and respect that is normally accorded for middle-class persons. But unless there are strong visible indications to the contrary, a black is held to have a lower-class style. He is, therefore, treated with the lack of deference and respect in the manner that is considered proper for dealing with persons of low status. To quote Drake: "the character of the Black Ghetto is not set by the newer 'gilded,' not-yet run-down portions of it, but by the older sections where unemployment rates are high and the masses of people work with their hands. . . ." [25] This kind of stereotyping on the basis of class blurs the actual status distinctions within each racial group and reinforces racial solidarities. It tends to mitigate the manifestation of antagonism between the different classes of whites or between the different classes of blacks.

As race and class once combined in American black servitude to form a unique social group, today their combined effects in the urban setting are creating another distinct element—*the black underclass*. The members of this class receive the worst of everything: the worst housing, the worst and most ineffectual schools, the worst jobs. The only thing they receive a disproportionately high share of is unemployment and disease. They are subject to control and exploitation by merchants, law, and police. Their welled-up frustrations are allowed to explode inward on themselves and their kind—just as long as it does not reach outward to their oppressors.

[25] St. Clair Drake, "The Social and Economic Status of the Negro in the United States," *Daedalus*, Fall, 1965, p. 777.

Concessions to their interests are primarily short-run benefits for survival purposes. Rarely are concessions granted which would change their status in the long-run. Public welfare, public housing, and low level patronage jobs, for example, keep the black underclass from starvation and exposure. At the same time, such benefits are so structured as to bring about dependency and degradation. In contrast, the subsidies granted to other strata are considered rights.[26] All these forces combine to make the black underclass a group without influence, subject to manipulation, and without legitimate means of redressing their grievances.

The consolidation of the black underclass has been clearly demonstrated during the big economic boom of the sixties. Every other group has been able to improve its income and conditions during this period. Middle-class and stable working-class blacks have been able to improve their income and housing. Poor whites in the metropolis have been able to better their conditions. But a very large sector of the urban black population has not received economic gains midst this prosperity. Therefore many in the stable black working-class fear being shoved back down into this underclass status in the advent of a depression.

The existence and the growth of the black underclass works to frustrate strategies of middle-class assimilation into the mainstream of white America. "Trickle down" approaches are not effective when rigid status barriers prevent the "trickle" from getting down far enough. On the other hand, the bonds of race are so strong in American society that there is no black man, regardless of how great his personal prestige, who can successfully disassociate himself from his brother in the black underclass.[27]

[26] Homeowners receive housing subsidies in the form of income tax abatements in which the higher the income, the greater the rate of subsidy. The oil companies receive subsidies in depletion allowances. That great Democrat from Mississippi, Senator Eastland, receives over $100,000 a year in cotton subsidies. None of these groups are stigmatized for being dependent on government handouts.

[27] This sentiment is well expressed by Dr. Percy Julian, renowned scientist, man of culture and wealth, resident in a white suburb, who wrote to a Chicago newspaper to document this point. He spoke of his bitterness in experiencing expressions of white backlash and then added:

A second depressing experience recently was to cast off my role as a comfortable, respected scientist and, dressed in work clothes and

A tenacious heritage of racist ideology provides intellectual and symbolic unity for all these separate institutional elements. This ideology not only justifies the way things are, but also serves as a framework for setting of new goals and solving of problems. In this manner, it operates as a regulator of behavior. The ideology of racism has been a major feature of the American tradition at least since the eighteenth century. It has become so well established that it has a life of its own that is somewhat autonomous of the social conditions that it rationalizes.

In America, the dominant theme of racist ideology has been to blame blacks for their own subjugation. The early American theorists on race held that blacks were brutish—physically, morally, and mentally incapable of self-determining independence. Therefore, it was both just and to his advantage that he be a slave. In recent years, the more sophisticated and paternalistic manifestations of the theory do not use rationales based on biological inheritance. They develop schemas of social causation in which certain aspects of fifty blacks' social life become the main determinants of their own subordinated condition. The "culturally deprived child" as the explanation for lack of academic success and Daniel P. Moynihan's position on the pathological Negro family are two recent examples of this kind of reasoning.

A secondary theme in the ideology of racism has been that the advantages for the dominant group are positive enough on their own account to justify the subjection of the black man. A master theoretician of the slave system, John C. Calhoun, claimed on the floor of the United States Senate "that there has never yet existed a wealthy and civilized society in which one portion of the community did not, in fact, live on the labor of the other." [28] In crude

---

shoes and an old cap, to walk and drive through the streets to see again just how "an ordinary Negro" is treated. I shall never forget the abuse, cursing and indignities heaped upon me as I "accidentally" made a few harmless mistakes. I discovered again why Stokely Carmichael gets cheers from young Negro youngsters and Negro mobs. Painfully, I realized that there is a bit of Stokely Carmichael in nearly every American Negro, even in me. I had almost forgotten that I was once an angry man. (*Chicago Tribune,* No. 11, 1967.)

[28] "Speech on the Reception of the Abolition Petitions," reprinted in Eric McKitrick, ed., *Slavery Defended: the Views of the Old South* (Englewood Cliffs, New Jersey: Prentice-Hall, Inc., 1963), p. 13.

forms the champions of the "white race" still propound this rationale. Such atavisms, however, do not represent the major operating force of this theme today. As we shall note later, its heritage largely provides the framework within which competing priorities are judged. When the interests of blacks are in opposition to those of some other group, the blacks are almost invariably forced to give way under the rationale that it is for the "good of the entire community" or it is necessary for the socially justified needs of some highly valued institution.

The force of the doctrine of racism in guiding and justifying the course of this nation has been sadly underrated. The coherent doctrine that was once embodied in constitutional law through the *Dred Scott* and *Plessy* vs. *Ferguson* decisions is now somewhat ragged. The so-called scientific defenses of it are few today. Yet, it is still ever present in a fragmented form, framing the assumptions that go into the analysis of particular problems. The assumptions, of course, largely determine the solutions offered. The retention of an ideology that is fundamentally racist has much to do with the ineffectiveness of most of the programs that have been labeled "antipoverty" and "antiracist."

Cui Bono?

Racism had its birth in slavery's exploitation. The massive and monolithic system of the southern plantation was erected upon this base. As Thomas Dew, Professor at William and Mary College and one of slavery's defenders, wrote, "it's, in truth, the slave labor in Virginia which gives value to her soil and her habitations; take away this, and you pull down the Atlas that upholds the whole system; eject from the States the whole slave population . . . and the Old Dominion will be a waste howling wilderness. . . ." [29] In the southern plantation system, both before and after slavery, economic exploitation of blacks was obvious. The planter class justified it, because the whole socioeconomic structure rose or fell on that relationship.

[29] "Review of the Debates in the Virginia Legislature" in McKitrick, ed., *op. cit.*, p. 20.

It is equally obvious that the capitalistic system as embodied in the modern urban United States does not rise or fall on the economic exploitation of American blacks. Western European nations with similar socioeconomic structures function without subjugated domestic black populations. While it is true that the present-day urban corporate nature of American society could endure without an elaborate structure of urban racism, there are still many groups and individuals who reap direct advantage from the exploitation of blacks. Therefore, in the answer to the question *cui bono,* for whose benefit, it must be said that there is a fragmentation of interest in the exploitative aspects of urban racism. No single ruling group like the plantocracy is economically dependent upon racial exploitation, but a multitude of small secondary groups are making direct gain out of racism. In addition, large numbers of whites derive indirect advantages.

The direct kinds of exploitation involve economic gains that are realizable through manipulation of the restricted and subordinated positions blacks occupy in various market relationships. In the housing market, blacks pay a premium or a color tax for the restricted supply that exists in the ghetto. Some real estate traders become specialized to this type of market and have developed sophisticated techniques for capitalizing on this advantage. In the labor market, certain firms have come to specialize in a black labor force, especially in particular semiskilled and unskilled occupations. Since the black worker is, on the average, paid less than the comparable white worker, these employers gain an advantage by paying less for the same quality of labor. Merchants operating in the ghetto often charge more for goods and credit or sell inferior-quality merchandise at regular prices. Obviously, those who own businesses that are specialized to a black market or a black labor force have a certain stake in the status quo, just to maintain their accustomed mode of operation and profits. The extra advantages gained by racial exploitation in wages or prices tend to give these firms and individuals an added stake in the maintenance of the overall racial system.

The indirect elements of exploitation are more varied and of greater importance. In addition to the economic form, social, psychological, and political types of exploitation also take place. Many white individuals and groups measure their own superiority on the basis that they rank higher in status than blacks. This social worth is manifested to them in that there is someone further down on the ladder. Very often, such enhancement of social worth serves as a mask for privilege in access to preferred employment. In varying ways, depending on social status and the nature of the situation, whites can feel that they are victors because they are relating to victimized blacks. These psychological and social gains, although invidious, are quite real. In the political realm, black people are utilized for other's ends. While blacks are enfranchised in urban areas, their voting strength is so hemmed in that they usually have to settle for minor political concessions and token representation.

These elements of racial exploitation, dispersed as they may be within white society, weigh heavily in the lives of black men. Exploitation robs the black of income and extorts a tribute in the purchase of food and shelter. The psychic or economic gains to whites might not form a big portion of the total for them, but the advantages have become an accepted part of the balance in urban society. Therefore, the elimination of these gains tends to disturb the equilibrium and engender strong forces to restore the old balance. Much of the resistance to racial change must be seen as the defense of real or perceived benefits on the part of whites.

MAINTAINING THE BALANCE

In the modern metropolitan setting, the basic wealth of the dominant white sectors is not dependent upon the economic exploitation of blacks. The top leadership of the white groups is not constrained to make its fundamental choices in terms of extracting direct advantage from blacks. Accordingly, there is much less articulation of a diehard defense of racism as a system by business and political leadership today. Under the pressure of black discontent, these groups are more and more characterized by a rhetoric of racial amelioration. In contrast to the Old South, subjugated blacks are not a requisite to make the present system work. However, since black people just will not disappear, society must contend with them.

But white society does not exist as a homogeneous mass. It is highly structured, especially as regards the control of power and the ownership of productive wealth. A relatively small number of corporations and bureaucracies have at their disposition the major share of the nation's resources. These dominant institutions of modern America are controlled by the propertied class and their increasingly necessary allies, the technocratic elites. However, in a modern democratic state such institutional control is not transferable directly into overall control of the society. It is mediated through a very complex set of working relationships and concessions with other social strata and groupings—sometimes worked out informally and sometimes worked out explicitly through local, state or national politics. The complicated social and political processes of this mediation exist in balance with the more structured aspects of basic control. Sometimes one gives way to the other, but together they form a total system. Given the fundamental racism of American society what we find is that even though racial exploitation is no longer an essential element in terms of sustaining a sector of a ruling class, racial dominance has become so socially diffused that it has become an inextricable part of the mediating processes through which much of the basic economic and political controls for the whole society are exercised. In other words, the mechanisms for subjugating black people have become interlaced with the complex of mechanisms by which power is exercised over both white and black. A root and branch abolition of racism, therefore, threatens the power order as we now know it. This is the fundamental political dynamic behind the institutional maintenance of racism.

The political balance of urban America is so easily thrown out of kilter by racial changes precisely because racism is so prevalent in the institutional life of the city. There exists a black community in the cities which contains in its status structure a unique and growing underclass. Blacks function in the total society basically through their participation in the black subsectors of the major institutional operation. Some whites directly gain an exploitative advantage out of racial subordination. Most of the whites partially define their prestige and self-esteem by their insulation from the black subsectors (i.e., not always by their distance from individual blacks). Finally, effective equality for blacks would require major rechanneling of public expenditures and shifts in power relationships. In other words, massive changes for blacks cannot occur without massive changes among whites. With the growing size of the urban black population, the unique position of the black underclass, and the historic entrenchment of racism, it is difficult to make major racial alterations and at the same time to continue the status quo relationships of whites vis-à-vis whites. Given these conditions, established leadership has made as its first priority the maintenance of equilibrium and control within the white sector. Reforms or concessions for blacks are limited by the prior consideration of not upsetting the white applecart.

The history of urban renewal offers an excellent illustration of this manner of choosing between competing racial objectives. Urban renewal has generally been used to create geographic and social insulation from the ghetto for prestigious institutions, especially downtown business districts and major universities. In order for these institutions to maintain their present operating efficiency and prestige, the housing of many black families was bulldozed. Displaced families were thrown into a segregated housing market with a limited and poor supply of housing. The urban renewal decisions were not made for the primary purpose of controlling or exploiting blacks. They were made for institutions which basically service whites and ignore blacks. These major institutions felt that the nearby presence of the ghetto, especially the proximity of poor blacks, threatened the socially justified continuation of their traditional operation. Therefore, the housing needs of blacks were subordinated to the perceived needs for continuity of these prestigious operations. The traditional stability of white institutions was maintained by pushing black families around.

Similar examples can be drawn from the spheres of politics, education, and employment. In politics, blacks are asked, in the name of party unity, to cease pressing for their just demands for fear of white backlash. In education, blacks are asked to be glad to have classrooms that are a little less crowded instead of the reorganization of the school system which would really provide their children with an education. In employment, blacks are barred from foremanships because harmony in the white work force is bolstered by various ethnic formulas for advancement into these jobs. This overall situation provides much of the basis for the growing concern of civil rights and black organizations with questions as to the manner in which the entire society operates.

In response to the growing pressures from the black community, the established authorities so far have developed two major strategies of reaction which conform to the priority of maintaining white equilibrium. First, there is the absorption of some better-trained, middle-class blacks into white organizations at a rate that is not greater than the going tolerance for tokenism in the given institution. Secondly, the social and physical isolation of the mass of blacks is bolstered, either in an ameliorative fashion by an increase in paternalistic type welfare programs, or in a repressive fashion by open rejection and naked violence.

THE COMMUNITY BEYOND

W. E. B. DuBois long ago told us that "the problem of the twentieth century was the problem of the color line." This essay has traced that line into the modern metropolis. In the colorless language of the social scientist, it has been a study in the urban system of racial controls. In the course of concentrating on the racial barriers, little could be said of the people hemmed in by them. The walls a society erects can proscribe a man, but they never can fully define a man. Therefore, the reader should not mistake this essay for an analysis of the black man in the city. It merely details the boundaries within which he lives and operates.

The constrictions of the color line have made the black's life in America a trying one. DuBois used the metaphor that it was like living behind a veil—*in* but not *of* the society. He wrote:

> One ever feels his twoness—an American, a Negro; two souls, two thoughts, two unreconciled strivings; two warring ideals in one dark body, whose dogged strength alone keeps it from being torn asunder.
>
> The history of the American Negro is the history of this strife—this longing to attain self-conscious manhood, to merge his double self into a better and truer self. In this merging, he wishes neither

of his older selves to be lost. He would not Africanize America, for
America has too much to teach the world and Africa. He would not
bleach his Negro soul in a flood of white Americanism, for he knows
that Negro blood has a message for the world.[30]

Many of the liberal commentators on the race questions would
deny Negroes the validity of Du Bois' darker self. From Myrdal to
Moynihan, there has been a tendency to picture the black subculture
as pathological. These commentators see the damage wrought by oppression without being able to recognize the strength born amidst
suffering. Such judgments rest upon the assumption that the dominant white society which exercises racism's controls, is the healthy
organism into which the sick ghetto should dissolve. As they over-
emphasize the health of a racist society, they are compelled to see
little but pathology in the life of its victims. Black culture and
personality are depicted one-sidedly in terms of the scars of oppression. Furthermore, the black man and his milieu are defined purely
in terms of reaction to the white world. It is as though the truth of
the general proposition that "man makes his own history" is granted,
but in this case its special form as "the white man makes the black
man's history." Thereby, the value, creativity, and potential of the
black *qua* black is denied.

Black writers were aware of this point long before the current
surge of black consciousness. In an unpublished review of Myrdal's
An American Dilemma, Ralph Ellison wrote in 1944: "But can a
people live and develop for three hundred years simply by *reacting*?
Are American Negroes simply the creation of white men, or have
they at least helped to create themselves out of what they found
around them? Men have made a way of life in caves and upon
cliffs, why cannot Negroes have made a life upon the horns of the
white man's dilemma?"[31]

There can be no question that the constrictions of racist controls
have brought torment to life in the ghetto. The pressures upon its
individuals and institutions have been so terrific that many have
bent or broken under them. None have gone totally untouched. But
one must also recognize the social and cultural bonds forged amidst

[30] W. E. B. DuBois, *The Souls of Black Folk* (Connecticut: Fawcet
Publishing Company, various editions).
[31] *Shadow and Act* (New York: Signet Edition 1, 1966), p. 301.

the travail of the black man's life behind the veil. A distinctive style of life with its own strengths and weaknesses has developed there; today, far from dying out, it appears to be becoming more cohesive. In their preface to the 1962 edition of *Black Metropolis* the authors concluded: "The family, clique and associational structures of Negroes in Chicago have been little affected by the trend toward 'integration.' . . . *Changes have been in the direction of a more intensive elaboration of Bronzeville's separate sub-culture, not toward its disappearance.*" [32]

This finding has been recently underscored by the upsurge of national identification and the redefinition of self-concepts under the slogans of "black pride" and "black consciousness." Blacks are now seeking to find their roots positively in their own subculture before they face the rest of America and the world. They are forging the social instrumentalities for their own self-determination.

The urban ghetto is destructive to the extent that it forms a prison for the Negroes' minds and bodies. It exists cancerously as the base upon which the *Herrenvolk* tradition of white American culture rests. *Since contradictions abound in reality, the ghetto boundaries are also those of a black community in which resides a proud and vigorous people. For the black man, his human identity, art and song, joy and sorrow, triumph and tragedy, are all rooted in this communion.* Within these bounds lie the strength and will to purge the body politic—to rid America of the crippling grip of racism. The contradiction of destruction and creation residing together cannot be wished away. Hopefully, it can be resolved into new and liberating social forms. Surely no more powerful force for such a change exists than that of the increasingly self-conscious black people. They truly have become the vanguard of the American future.

White men and black men are locked together in this nation so that they determine one another's fate. Since the day has come when the darker brother will no longer suffer trustingly like Job, a new destiny awaits both white and black. Racism's cancer, disturbed by the resistance, can feed upon itself and bring greater

---

[32] St. Clair Drake and Horace Cayton, *Black Metropolis: A Study of Negro Life in a Northern City*, Volume II (New York and Evanston: Harper and Row, Inc., 1962), ii, xiii.

destruction in its wake. Or, the healthy elements in the two cultures can contend and react upon each other, creatively transforming both their institutions and their individuals in the process. The one possibility denied to each culture is to operate in isolation as though the other were not there.

Index